ENCYCLOPEDIA OF CATS

ENCYCLOPEDIA OF CATS

JULIANNA PHOTOPOULOS

Copyright © 2024 Amber Books Ltd

All rights reserved. No part of this publication may be reproduced, stored in a retrieval system, or transmitted in any form or by any means, electronic, mechanical, photocopying, recording, or otherwise, without prior written permission of the copyright holder.

Published by
Amber Books Ltd
United House
North Road
London N7 9DP
United Kingdom

ISBN: 978-1-83886-445-3

www.amberbooks.co.uk
Facebook: amberbooks
YouTube: amberbooksltd
Instagram: amberbooksltd
X(Twitter): @amberbooks

Project Editor: Anna Brownbridge
Designer: Keren Harragan and Andrew Easton
Picture Research: Adam Gnych

Printed in China

Contents

Introduction	6
Shorthair	8
Fur	70
Nose, Mouth & Paws	98
Claws	100
Eyes	164
Vision	166
Mating & Fighting	244
Fighting & Aggression	246
Longhair	290
Tongue	308
Grooming	310
Whiskers	362
Senses	364
Ears	408
Index	446
Picture Credits	448

Introduction

T HE DEVELOPMENT OF CAT BREEDS began in the mid-19th century when like-minded cat owners began to form clubs and put on shows and competitions. Unlike domesticated dogs, cats have not changed much genetically from their wild predator ancestor, the African wildcat (*Felis lybica*), since they were never bred for specific tasks such as hunting or herding. Today, many breed organisations exist and the number of cat breeds and varieties, as well as breed names and characteristics, or standards, differ among them.

Broadly divided into shorthairs and longhairs, there are over 100 cat breeds and varieties, defined by their appearance: coat colour and pattern, head and body shape, and eye colour. Some also have unusual traits, such as folded or curled ears, wavy coats, or even no tail or fur, and their size and temperament differ. With 700 million cats living worldwide, domestic cats – also known as *Felis catus* – are one of the most popular companion pets. However, not all domestic cats are of a particular breed and, in fact, the majority of pets have unknown or mixed ancestry.

OPPOSITE:
Tiffanie
This adorable semi-longhaired kitten is a gentle, cuddly cat that loves to spend time with its family.

Shorthair

Like their wild predator ancestor, most cats have short, sleek coats that do not typically grow longer than about 4cm (1.5in). This allows them to move more freely and slowly approach, or stalk, their prey until they powerfully pounce on it – even in a tight corner. Many modern cat breeds with short coats have been developed within the last two centuries. In a short coat, these cats have well-defined, often muscular, bodies that give them an athletic appearance. They can come in a wide variety of coat colours and distinct patterns, as well as distinctive features and personalities. In some cases, short hair has been taken to the extreme, like in hairless breeds such as the Sphynx. These cats are usually not completely hairless but have a very fine fuzz-like coat as a result of a natural mutation. Other unique coat features caused by genetic mutations are curly or wavy coats, as seen in rexed cats, such as the Cornish Rex or Devon Rex. Shorthairs are generally easier to maintain because they require less grooming. However, each breed is unique and still needs attention to look and feel its best.

OPPOSITE:
American Burmese
The American Burmese breed can be distinguished from its similar European relative by its stockier build and broader head.

SHORTHAIR
Abyssinian

One of the most popular breeds, the Abyssinian was developed in the United Kingdom, with records dating back to the 1890s. But its exact origins remain somewhat of a mystery. Some people believe Abyssinians are the direct descendants of the sacred cats of ancient Egyptians, while others suggest they originated in Abyssinia – what is now Ethiopia – and travelled alongside British soldiers to England. One of these cats from Ethiopia is said to be Zula, who won first prize in the 1871 Crystal Palace cat show. However, genetic research has shown that Abyssinians may have originated near the coast of the Indian Ocean. Regardless of where the Abyssinian hailed from, the modern breed is wildly captivating with its almond-shaped eyes, large ears and distinctive ticked coat, where each hair has alternate bands of dark and light colours called 'agouti'. Active and curious, the Abyssinian is constantly on the move and spends most of its day following its owners around, playing, climbing or exploring every nook and cranny – anything to not sit still but always in the company of others!

CHARACTERISTICS

Coat
Several colours with distinct ticking pattern
Weight
2.7–5.4kg (6–12lbs)
Lifespan
12–16 years
Personality
Energetic, intelligent, playful
Origin
Coasts of the Indian Ocean / United Kingdom

ABOVE:
Usual-coloured
An Abyssinian looks wild in this classic reddish-brown coat with black ticking, known as 'usual' or 'ruddy'.

RIGHT
Origins
The Abyssinian is named after Abyssinia (now Ethiopia) where it was believed to have originated.

SHORTHAIR

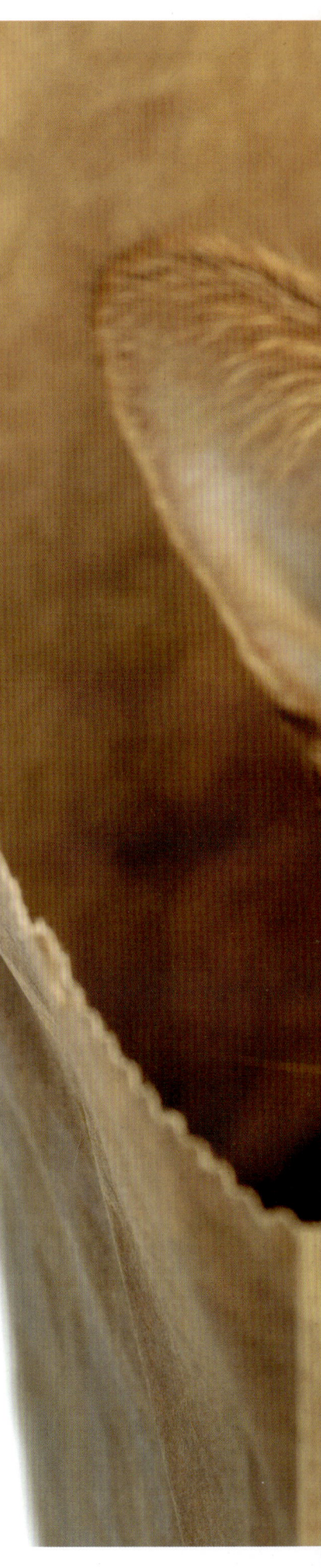

ABOVE:
Healthier kitties
The first cat to have its entire genome sequenced in 2007 was an Abyssinian named Cinnamon. This could help breed healthier cats.

RIGHT:
Playtime
This curious Abyssinian happily sits inside a paper bag. Paper bags can provide endless hours of fun for playful cats.

SHORTHAIR

SHORTHAIR

RIGHT:
Class clown
This energetic, curious and intelligent breed, often seeking to play with its owners, is also known as the 'clown of the cat kingdom'.

OPPOSITE:
Camouflage
This original-coloured Abyssinian, with its 'usual' coat pattern, looks wild. In fact, ticked fur provides camouflage to many wild cats and other mammals.

SHORTHAIR

ABOVE:
Wild look
American Bobtails can have either a short or a long coat in a variety of colours and patterns. However, the breed standard favours a 'wild' appearance which resembles a bobcat.

American Bobtail

CHARACTERISTICS

Coat
All colours and patterns, with or without white

Weight
3.2–7.3kg (7–16lb)

Lifespan
11–15 years

Personality
Affectionate, sociable, adaptable, intelligent

Origin
United States

This relatively large, muscular cat is known for its wild appearance and unusual short, or bobbed, tail. Its bobbed tail – about half-length or less than that of the average cat – is the result of a natural genetic mutation. And though these short-tailed cats existed in America for years, the American Bobtail wasn't developed until the late 1960s. The original bloodline was created from Yodie, a short-tailed brown tabby male found in Arizona. Since then, the American Bobtail comes in all colours and coat patterns, both in short-haired and long-haired varieties.

The American Bobtail is intelligent, loves to play games, such as fetch and hide-and-seek, but also enjoys quiet times. Due to its affectionate and friendly personality, it is often described as dog-like – it even wags its short tail to express its mood and walks on a lead! This breed easily adapts to almost any environment and gets along with everyone – even children, other pets and strangers – making them great pets in any household.

ABOVE:
Bobbed tail
The naturally occurring shortened tail gives the American Bobcat its name. At about 2.5–10cm (1–4in) long, the bobbed tail can be straight, slightly curved or kinked, or have bumps along its length.

Feline friends
These short-tailed kittens are playful, sociable and generally love travelling and being among people.

SHORTHAIR
American Burmese

As the name suggests, this breed of cat originated in Burma – now known as Myanmar. A female cat named Wong Mau was brought from Burma to the United States in the 1930s, where it was crossed with the Siamese, creating the American Burmese (also sometimes called contemporary Burmese). Burmese cats were also brought over and bred in the United Kingdom, where they developed a distinct look with a longer head and leaner body – now often referred to as the European Burmese. However, most cat registries do not recognise the American and European Burmese as separate breeds.

The American Burmese can be distinguished from its European relative by its stockier build and broader head. It also has rounder eyes, a shorter and flatter muzzle and ears that are wider at their base. Both varieties are medium-sized and often feel heavy due to their muscular build. Coat colours vary considerably and different colours are approved by the major cat organisations, making the Burmese standard one of the more complex among pedigreed domestic cats.

CHARACTERISTICS

Coat
CFA: Sable (solid black/ dark brown), champagne (chocolate), platinum (lilac), blue
TICA: All solid and tortie colours in sepia pattern

Weight
2.7–6.4 kg (6–14lb)

Lifespan
Up to 18 years

Personality
Social, playful, vocal

Origin
Possibly Burma (Myanmar) / United States

ABOVE:
Cat companions
Burmese cats require human company and attention.

RIGHT:
Distinctive traits
A chocolate American Burmese showing the distinctive wide-set, round, golden eyes and short, rounded muzzle.

SHORTHAIR

ALL PHOTOGRAPHS:
In need of attention
Contrary to the typical feline stereotype, the Burmese cat is not as independent as other breeds.

ABOVE:
Soft and sleek
Burmese cats have luxurious, satin-like fur that is lighter in colour on their underparts. This European Burmese has a longer head and muzzle than its American counterpart.

RIGHT:
Young cats
As they grow older, these European Burmese kittens will not lose their energy, playfulness or cuteness. However, they will look deceptively lighter than they actually are!

SHORTHAIR

American Curl

With distinctive big eyes and unusual ears, the first American Curls were long-haired. In fact, the breed's ancestor was a black long-haired female stray called Shulamith, who was discovered by a family in Southern California in 1981. But this unique trait of curled-back ears quickly gained interest from breeders and geneticists, and both long-haired and short-haired varieties were developed.

The fluffy ears of the American Curl – which ideally curl backwards between 90 and 180 degrees – are a result of a natural mutation. Kittens are born with straight ears that usually begin to curl within a few days up until kittens are about four months old. But it's not only the curled ears that make these cats so attractive. Affectionate and alert, American Curls form strong attachments to their family and easily adapt to children and other pets. They do not like to be left alone for too long and enjoy several hours of attention and playtime every day. These curious cats will even follow owners around the house, gently poke and prod with their paws, and give affectionate head bumps!

CHARACTERISTICS

Coat
All colours and patterns
Weight
2.3–4.5kg (5–10lb)
Lifespan
10-20 years
Personality
Curious, friendly, affectionate
Origin
United States

LEFT:
Young at heart
The American Curl, nicknamed 'Peter Pan of cats', keeps its kitten-like behaviour throughout its life.

ABOVE:
Unusual traits
Designer cat breeds with unusual traits, like the American Curl, are often expensive.

SHORTHAIR

Ear-resistible
The distinctive curled ears of American Curls appear within a week of birth in at least half of the litter. These adorable kittens have both curled and straight ears.

Daily exercise
American Curls have kitten-like personalities and need daily exercise; they love to play with toys, climb, jump and explore.

SHORTHAIR
American Shorthair

Formerly known as the Domestic Shorthair, this popular breed was renamed the American Shorthair in 1966 to represent its American roots and differentiate it from other shorthair breeds. It is believed to have originated from the first domestic cats brought by early pilgrims from Europe to the United States in the 1600s. American Shorthairs are sometimes called *working cats* since they were used to hunt rodents on farms and ships. And while they are not known for being athletic, all those years as hard-working mousers paid off and their bodies are surprisingly sturdy and powerful. These attractive cats have a thick, short coat that can have more than 80 different colours and patterns, often with bold stripes. Known to be highly adaptable and affectionate to children and other animals, American Shorthairs can thrive in any type of household – even in a busy one where they like to participate too!

CHARACTERISTICS
Coat
Most colours and patterns
Weight
2.7–6.8 kg (6–15lb)
Lifespan
15–20 years
Personality
Calm, friendly, easy-going, curious
Origin
United States

ABOVE:
Good looks
American Shorthairs have short noses and large, wide-set eyes that can be various colours, although green or gold are quite common.

RIGHT
Popular cat
The American Shorthair was the eighth most popular cat in the world in 2023, according to the Cat Fanciers' Association (CFA).

SHORTHAIR

Sweet kitty
This gentle and sweet cat tends to be a happy and playful pet but also has an independent streak.

SHORTHAIR

SHORTHAIR

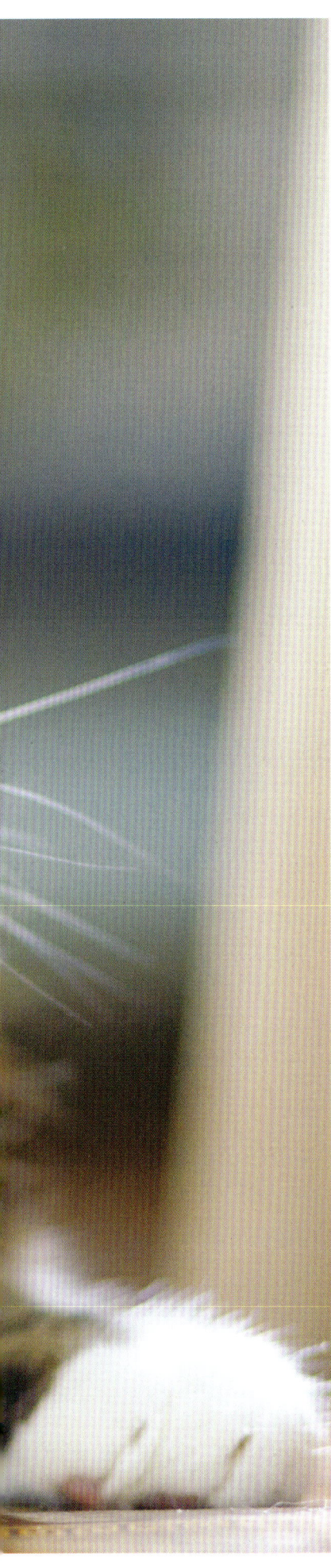

LEFT:
Pilgrim cat
This popular North American breed is said to have been on board the famous transatlantic voyage of the English sailing ship, *Mayflower*.

ABOVE:
Cute kittens
With rounded faces, these adorable kittens are known for being affectionate to children, dogs and other pets.

SHORTHAIR

ABOVE:
Hunting instinct
Like many cats, the American Wirehair will pounce at insects and gaze at birds with interest.

American Wirehair

CHARACTERISTICS

Coat
Many colours and patterns
Weight
3.6-6.8kg (8–15lb)
Lifespan
12–18 years
Personality
Calm, affectionate, curious
Origin
United States

Named after its springy and wiry coat, the first American Wirehair was discovered in a litter of kittens in Verona, New York, in 1966. The young male cat was spotted by a local breeder who noticed that all his hairs – including his whiskers – were crimped, which seemed unique. It was later revealed to be the result of a genetic mutation. The American Wirehair is a close relative of the American Shorthair: they are similar in looks and personality and the only difference between the two breeds is the wiriness of their coats. An American Wirehair's coat is dense overall but individual hairs can vary from spiked to curly. In some individuals, hairs may be hard and break easily, while in others they are more malleable and spring back into place when petted. American Wirehairs are gentle, quiet and friendly. They generally prefer to stay indoors, although some also feel at home outdoors. While this breed enjoys human company, and may even regularly curl up on someone's lap, they are also quite independent.

ABOVE:
Wiry hair
The genetic mutation that causes wiry hair is different from that found in other curly-coated breeds.

SHORTHAIR

RIGHT:
Calm kitty
This gentle, quiet and friendly wire-haired kitten is happy outdoors or indoors – though generally it prefers to stay indoors.

OPPOSITE:
Close relatives
The wirehair has a similar personality to its relative, the American shorthair, which was used to develop the breed.

SHORTHAIR

Aphrodite

Also known as Aphrodite's Giant, this large cat is being developed as a standardized breed from domesticated cats on the island of Cyprus, in both short-haired and long-haired versions. Cyprus cats have been breeding largely on their own for centuries, which has allowed them to become a distinct local cat variety. The earliest records of the Cyprus cats – dating back to AD 4 – describe how Saint Helena sent two boats full of these cats from Egypt or Palestine to a Cypriot monastery infested with snakes. It is believed that these cats once lived high up in the cold mountains, giving the Aphrodite its large, muscular body and somewhat thick coat. Affectionate and sociable, the Aphrodite loves being around the whole family, including children and other pets, which makes it a perfect family companion. It prefers to spend all day with owners, even sitting on their laps. Currently, it is recognized by the World Cat Federation (WCF) and provisionally recognized by The International Cat Association (TICA).

CHARACTERISTICS

Coat
All colours and patterns except mink and colourpoint
Weight
4.5–8.2kg (10–18lb)
Lifespan
12–15 years
Personality
Affectionate, gentle, sociable
Origin
Cyprus

ABOVE:
People-orientated
Though large and powerful, the Aphrodite is also elegant with a gentle and loving temperament, and wants to be close to people at all times.

RIGHT:
Seasonal coat
Native to Cyprus, the Aphrodite's coat varies by season: a soft cotton-woolly coat for winter and a shorter coat with no undercoat in the summer.

Caring cat
This exceptionally affectionate cat is best suited for a bustling family and quickly forms very strong bonds with all its members.

SHORTHAIR

SHORTHAIR

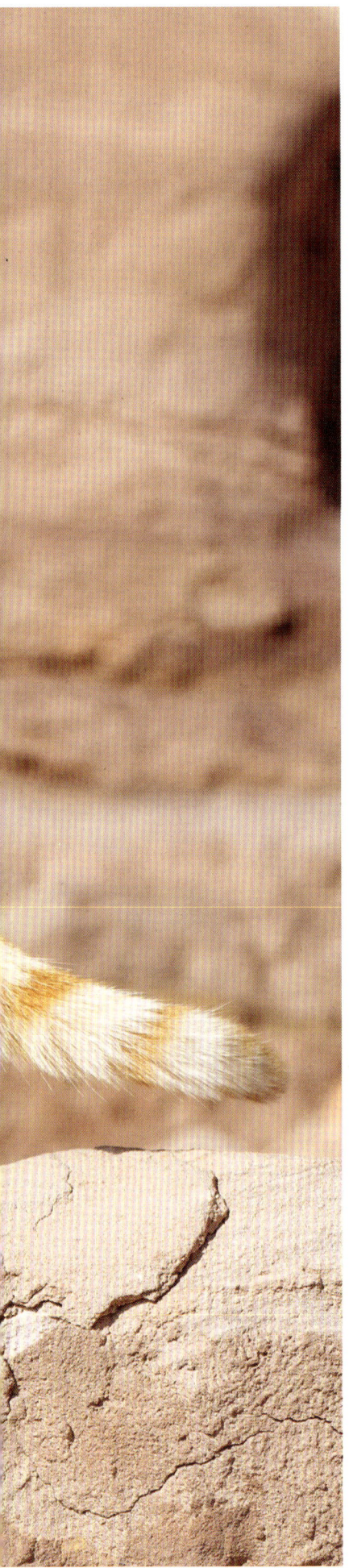

Arabian Mau

Once a desert cat in the Arabian Peninsula, the Arabian Mau moved towards human settlements in search of food as deserts became cities, and quickly became domesticated. A modern breed was developed in the 2000s to save its original features and qualities. The Arabian Mau has adapted well to the hot climate: it wears a short coat that requires little grooming and has distinctive large, pointed ears that help it release heat to keep cool and pick up the faint squeaks of its prey. Its medium-sized, muscular body atop its long legs with oval paws allows it to jump and run quick sprints. Although the Arabian Mau is exceptionally active and retains its hunting and territorial instincts, it is also loyal and makes a devoted house companion. These cats love people and demand ample attention, so they are not to be left alone. In 2008, the breed was recognized by the World Cat Federation (WCF).

CHARACTERISTICS

Coat
Various colours and patterns, including tabby and bicolour
Weight
3.2–6.8kg (7–15lb)
Lifespan
12–15 years
Personality
Active, curious, affectionate
Origin
Arabian Peninsula

LEFT:
Natural hunter
Quick and agile, the Arabian Mau is well adapted to desert life and has an innate ability to hunt for food.

ABOVE:
Arabian cat
Native to the Arabian Peninsula, this breed can be found roaming the streets of countries like the United Arab Emirates.

SHORTHAIR

Posing
This is an attractive breed with pointy ears and green, slightly slanted oval eyes.

SHORTHAIR

PREVIOUS PAGES AND RIGHT:
Elegant cats
This elegant, medium-sized cat can be found in many various colours and patterns, including brown tabby bicolour.

OPPOSITE:
Loyal companion
The Arabian Mau can be a handful with its high energy levels and need for mental stimulation, but it is also both loyal and affectionate.

SHORTHAIR
Australian Mist

Nine years in the making, the Australian Mist is the first and only pedigree cat developed in Australia. It was created in the 1970s, combining the Burmese and Abyssinian with domestic shorthairs. The first cats – initially known as the Spotted Mists – had spotted coats with ticking, making them look shaded, or like mist. However, as the breed developed, more coat patterns emerged, which led to its new name in 1998: the Australian Mist. Australian Mists now have spotted or marbled coats in seven distinct colours, which take about two years to develop. These easy-going cats are said to be affectionate and happiest when cuddled with their families. They get along with people of all ages and other pets, so fit in easily in any household. Australian Mists prefer to always be in the company of others and are perfect lap cats. The International Cat Association (TICA) recognized this breed in 2014 and the UK's Governing Council of the Cat Fancy (GCCF) followed in 2017.

CHARACTERISTICS
Coat
Spotted or marbled tabby in brown, blue, chocolate, lilac, gold, peach and caramel
Weight
3.6–6.8kg (8–15lb)
Lifespan
15–18 years
Personality
Affectionate, friendly, easy-going
Origin
Australia

ABOVE:
Friendly face
With its distinctive round head, broad nose and large, expressive green eyes, the attractive Australian Mist has a friendly face.

RIGHT
Misted appearance
The Australian Mist is noted for its unique coat pattern that has random ticking. This gives the cat a misted appearance, hence the name.

SHORTHAIR

ABOVE:
Energetic kitten
Lively as a kitten, the Australian mist is affectionate and happily lives indoors.

OPPOSITE:
Perfect breed
The Australian mist combines the breeder's favourite cats: Burmese, Abyssinian and domestic shorthairs. It is a very popular breed in Australia.

SHORTHAIR

ABOVE:
Personality
The hairless, short-legged Bambino is athletic and has a gentle but lively, outgoing and affectionate personality.

Bambino

CHARACTERISTICS

Coat
Hairless; all colours and patterns
Weight
2.3–4.1kg (5–9lb)
Lifespan
8–14 years
Personality
Affectionate, friendly, playful
Origin
United States

A cross between the hairless Sphynx and the short-legged Munchkin, this unusual-looking, rare breed was intentionally created in the United States in 2005. It is a perfect mix of its parent breeds: the distinctive looks of the Sphynx combined with the Munchkin's extremely short legs. It has a wedge-shaped head with large ears and eyes, and while it may look entirely naked, the Bambino is usually covered with exceptionally fine downy hair. Its wrinkled skin is said to feel like a warm supple suede. Despite its short legs, the sturdy and well-muscled Bambino is known for being strong and surprisingly agile. They love to play, run and climb. However, the lack of fur makes them vulnerable to sunburns, cold weather and injury, so the Bambino is best suited as an indoor pet. Fortunately, it loves to spend time with its family and is happy for some lap or cuddle time. An experimental dwarf breed, the Bambino is only recognized by the Rare and Exotic Feline Registry (REFR).

ABOVE:
Small child
This dwarf breed's name – derived from the Italian word for 'baby' or 'child' – is apt, it weighing up to about 4kg (9lb).

SHORTHAIR

Bambino
This unusual, experimental breed was created relatively recently in 2005.

SHORTHAIR

Bengal

With exotic looks to match its name, the Bengal was developed by breeding wild Asian leopard cats (*Felis bengalensis*) with domestic cats like the Egyptian Mau and Abyssinian. While there were previous attempts at crossing the leopard cat with short-haired domestic cats – even for scientific research on feline leukaemia – the Bengal was officially accepted as a new breed by The International Cat Association (TICA) in 1986. A Bengal is best known for its strikingly distinct markings on its soft coat, such as spots, rosettes and marbling. Some coats also have an iridescent sheen and the coats look glittery when sunlight touches them. But the Bengal has a personality that is as appealing as its appearance. Affectionate and intelligent, it enjoys being a part of a family and can get along with just about everyone. However, this cat is full of energy and constantly wants to climb, explore and play. Most Bengal cats are short-haired but there is also a long-haired variety known as Bengal Longhair or Cashmere Bengal. These, however, require regular, daily grooming – unlike their short-haired relatives.

CHARACTERISTICS

Coat
Short or long; spotted and marble classic tabby patterns in brown, blue, silver and snow

Weight
2.7–6.8kg (6–15lb)

Lifespan
12–20 years

Personality
Energetic, intelligent, affectionate

Origin
United States

ABOVE:
Innate hunter
The Bengal owes most of its looks and hunting abilities to the leopard cat. Like its ancestor, it can suddenly spring onto its prey!

RIGHT:
Loving cat
Despite their wild cat ancestry, Bengals are very affectionate to their owners and can sometimes be found sitting on laps – but only on their own terms.

SHORTHAIR

ABOVE:
Mascara markings
A Bengal can have horizontal striping, or 'mascara' markings, around its large, beautiful oval-shaped (yet almost round) eyes.

RIGHT:
Rosettes
Bengals are the only domestic cats with distinct rose-like markings called rosettes on their fur, which are similarly found on wild cats like leopards and jaguars.

SHORTHAIR

Bengal
This exotically marked coat belongs to a very energetic and beautiful hybrid, which was previously known as the leopardette.

Mother and child
A mother licks her kitten to groom and show affection. Despite their wild-cat ancestry, Bengals are very affectionate to their owners, too.

Fur

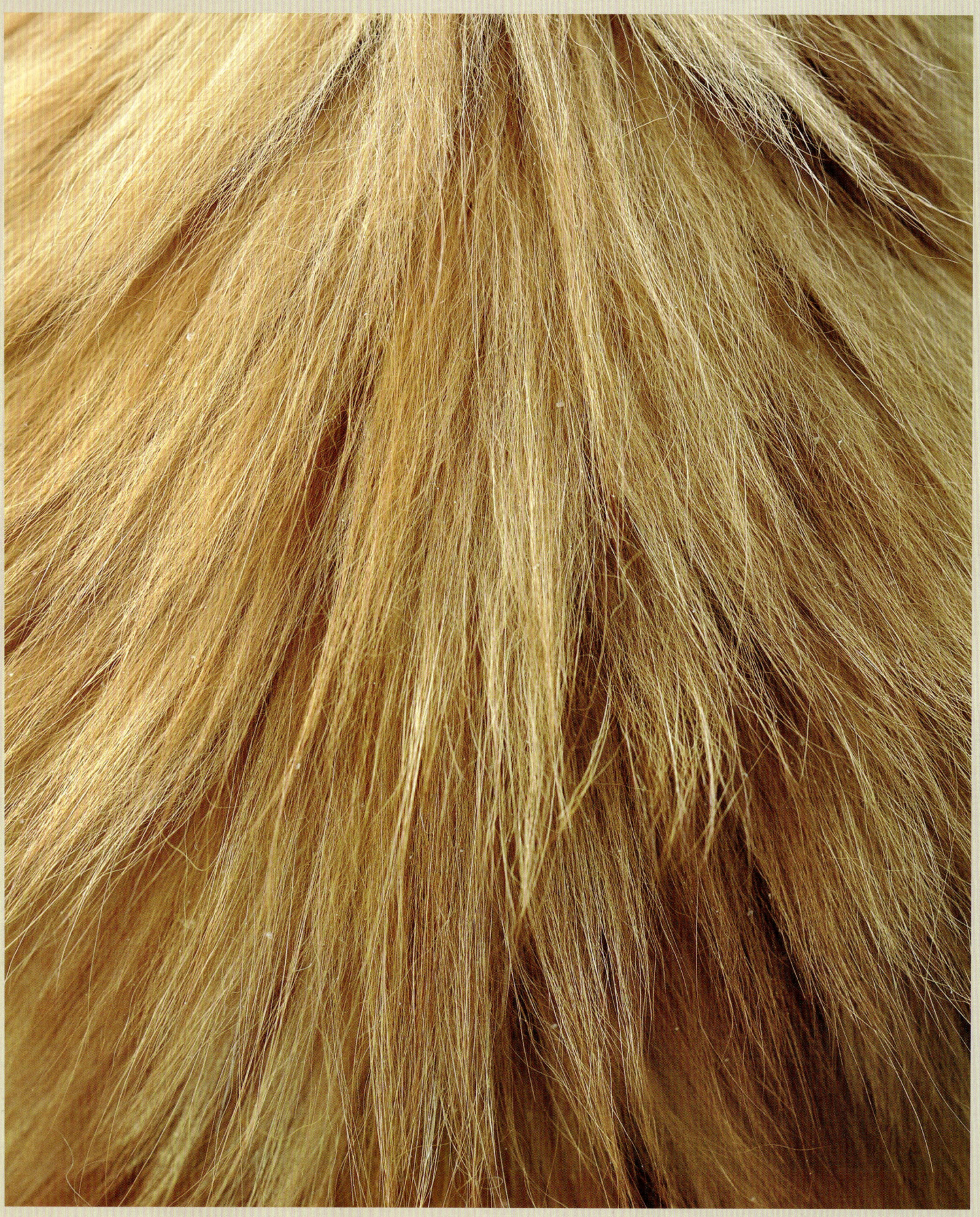

ALL PHOTOGRAPHS:
Cat coats
Cats can have short or long coats, or even be bald. Coat colours that are only one colour and are without any patterns are known as 'solid'. A coat pattern of stripes and swirls is called tabby, though it can also have spots, blotches or whorls. When a coat has multiple colours, such as orange, black and white, the pattern is called calico.

SHORTHAIR

ABOVE:
Pose for the camera
This is one of many attractive shorthairs with particualarly expressive eyes.

RIGHT:
Wild and free
The Brazilian Shorthair breed loves to explore both indoors and outdoors.

SHORTHAIR
British Shorthair

One of the larger cat breeds, this British favourite is thought to have originated from the cats of ancient Rome. These cats were brought by the Romans to the United Kingdom to keep down vermin and are said to have later interbred with the native wild cats. By the late 19th century, the best British domestic cats were bred with each other to develop the British Shorthair – one of the first breeds to appear in the first ever cat show at Crystal Palace in 1871. However, the British Shorthair had become very rare by the end of World War II, so breeders re-created and refined these cats by crossing them with other breeds, such as Russian Blues, Burmese and Persians.

Today, the stocky British Shorthair has a distinctive round head, with round cheeks, and large, round eyes. The males are significantly larger than the females, though both reach their full size at about three years old. Calm and quietly affectionate, British Shorthairs are wonderful companions, without being too demanding or hyperactive, and are accepting of strangers, considerate children and other pets. However, they are not keen on being picked up and prefer to be quietly near owners – even lounging on your laptop as you work!

CHARACTERISTICS

Coat
Many colours and patterns
Weight
3.2–7.7kg (7–17lb)
Lifespan
14–20 years
Personality
Affectionate, easy-going, calm
Origin
United Kingdom

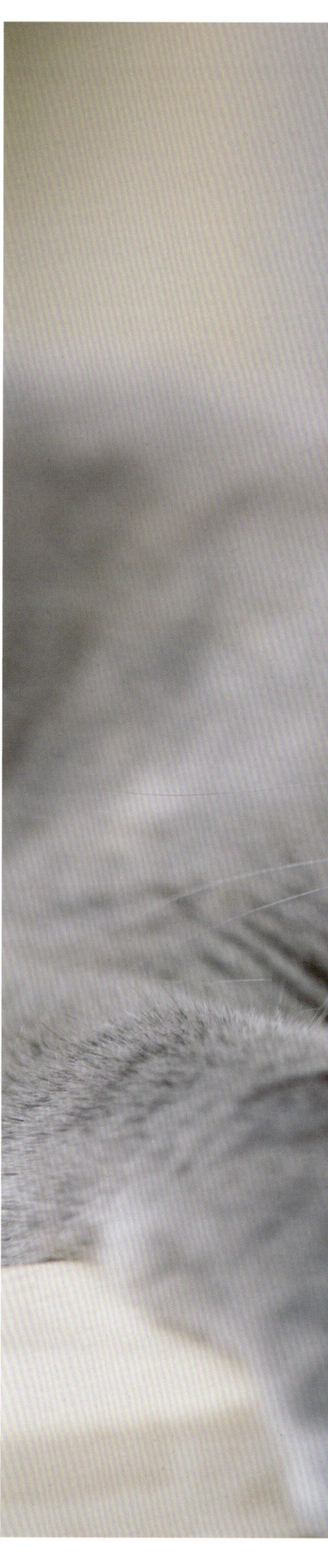

ABOVE:
Cheshire Cat
The British Shorthair is thought to have inspired the Cheshire Cat illustrations in Lewis Carroll's book, *Alice's Adventures in Wonderland*.

RIGHT:
British Blue
This magnificent breed is most popular in a blue-grey coat, known as the British Blue, but also comes in many other colours and patterns.

SHORTHAIR

ABOVE TOP:
Eye colour
All British Shorthair kittens are born with blue eyes, but their eye colour starts to develop at about 6 weeks. The blue eyes of this cuddly kitten will gradually turn copper, orange or deep gold.

ABOVE BOTTOM:
Crisp coat
This male, with a *crisp* coat and the distinct heavy jowls, licks its lips after eating. British Shorthairs are noted for their dense, *crisp* coat that breaks noticeably over their bodies as they move.

RIGHT:
Loudest purr
British Shorthairs are known to be quiet, but a British Shorthair called Smokey holds the Guinness World Record for the loudest purr by a domestic cat, measuring 67.8dB – as loud as a lawnmower!

Lounging around
This is one of the most ancient cat breeds, with many distinct colours and patterns.

Quiet kitten
British shorthairs are quietly affectionate and prefer to stay near their owners rather than sit on their laps or be picked up.

SHORTHAIR

ABOVE:
Sparkling silver
Burmilla cats are renowned for their stylish silver coat of fur.

Burmilla

CHARACTERISTICS

Coat
Short or long; various shaded or tipped colours, with silver or golden ground colour
Weight
3.6-6.8kg (8–15lb)
Lifespan
15–18 years
Personality
Fun-loving, playful, affectionate
Origin
United Kingdom

This captivating breed originated from the accidental mating of a Persian Chinchilla and a Burmese in the United Kingdom in 1981. The resulting litter was made up of four female kittens that were silver-coloured with short hair. Another distinguishing feature was the dark contours around their nose, lips and eyes which looked like make-up. Since the young cats were found to be attractive, a breeding programme ensued. Burmilla cats now come in various colours in shaded or tipped patterns, which means they have a darker or lighter colour covering their silver or golden coats – though only a few breed organizations recognize the latter.

The Burmilla is often considered to exhibit the best personality traits from its two parent breeds. It loves attention yet is not as demanding as the Burmese and tends to be more laid-back like the Persian – though it has inherited the mischievous streak from the Burmese too! Good-natured and affectionate, the Burmilla is ideal for families as it is happy to play with children and rarely says no to a lap cuddle.

ABOVE:
Asian Shaded
The Burmilla is sometimes also called Asian Shaded since certain cat registries consider it part of the Asian breed.

LEFT:
Green eyes
This breed has distinctive green eyes but the colour can vary in shade. Kittens and young adults may have a yellow tinge.

ABOVE TOP:
Nap time
Like all cats, the Burmilla sleeps about 12–18 hours a day. However, it also enjoys having fun with its owners.

ABOVE BOTTOM:
Relaxing
The easy-going Burmilla cat was a result of an accidental mating between a lilac Burmese and a Persian Chinchilla in 1981.

SHORTHAIR

California Spangled

With a long, lean and muscular body and a distinctive spotted coat, this designer cat was created in the 1970s to look like a miniature leopard. The breeders believed that, if people had a pet that resembled a wild cat, it would raise their awareness of the poaching trade and discourage them from buying and wearing fur coats. California Spangled cats were developed by crossing several domestic breeds, including the Abyssinian, Siamese, and American and British Shorthairs. They were introduced to the public in 1986 and were originally sold to raise funds to protect endangered wild cats in Central and South America. However, the popularity of two other exotic cats with spots – the Ocicat and the Bengal – overshadowed their development and these beautiful cats remain extremely rare. Despite its wild appearance, the California Spangled is completely domestic and adores playing and interacting with its family. It can often be found hunting, perching in high places or showing off its acrobatic skills. Due to its rarity, this breed is no longer recognized by any major breed organization.

CHARACTERISTICS

Coat
Spotted tabby in various colours, including black, brown and silver
Weight
4.1–6.8kg (9–15lb)
Lifespan
9–16 years
Personality
Active, affectionate, sociable
Origin
United States

ABOVE:
Spot shapes
The California Spangled has distinct spots on its coat which can be round, blocked, oval, square or triangular.

RIGHT:
House leopard
The almond-shaped eyes, high-set ears, wide cheekbones and prominent whisker pads top off this house leopard's look.

Chartreux

With a captivating woolly blue-grey coat and orange-coloured eyes, the quiet Chartreux from France often appears to be smiling. Legend has it that these cats were initially brought to France by Carthusian monks, makers of the Chartreuse liqueur, who kept them to keep mice and rats at bay. It is also said that the early ancestors of the Chartreux were feral mountain cats from Syria, brought to French monasteries by the returning Crusaders in the 13th century. Nevertheless, while prized for their hunting skills, Chartreux cats also became popular for their good looks and calm, undemanding demeanour. In fact, these exceptionally well-mannered cats rarely make any noise, and when they do, they chirp and trill. Since they get along with just about anyone and do not mind being left alone, Chartreux cats make excellent companions for individuals and families. Interestingly, they even enjoy travelling with their owners – quite unusual for cats!

CHARACTERISTICS

Coat
Blue-grey only

Weight
3.2–7.3kg (7–16lb)

Lifespan
11–15 years

Personality
Calm, affectionate, quiet

Origin
France

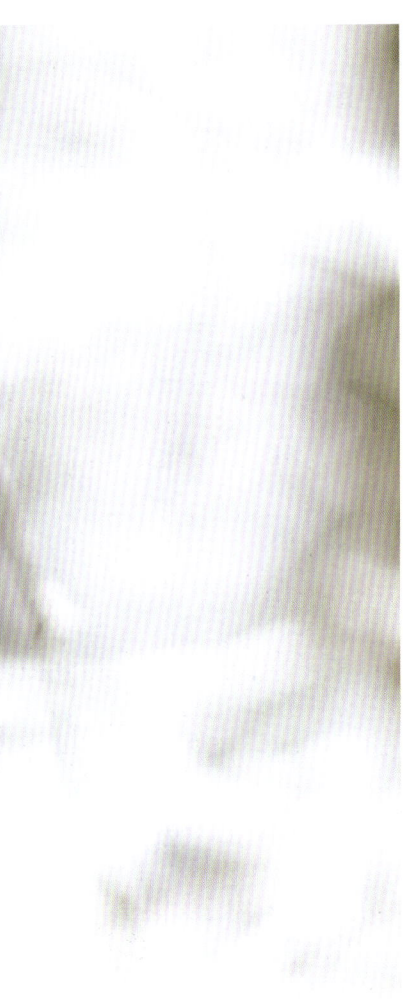

LEFT:
Woolly coat
Possibly named after the luxurious Spanish wool *pile des Chartreux*, the Chartreux has a woolly coat that protects it against cold and wet weather.

ABOVE:
Smiling expression
A national treasure in France, the Chartreux cat has a round head with full cheeks and a tapering muzzle which gives it a smiling expression.

SHORTHAIR

Young cats
These playful kittens that appear to be 'smiling' take about two years to reach adulthood.

Nose Mouth & Paws

OPPOSITE TOP & BOTTOM:
Smell
A cat's sense of smell is 14 times better than ours. Smell helps cats recognize people, objects, other cats or animals, and track their prey. Cats also use and leave smells for mating or to mark their territory and keep other cats away.

ABOVE:
Paw pads
Cat paws have a cushion-like pad under them to soften landings when they leap or jump off high places. These pads also help cats walk on rough ground and move and hunt quietly.

LEFT:
Natural cleaning
Cats start off cleaning themselves by licking their lips and paws. Their saliva contains a natural detergent-like substance that removes any scent and helps keep their fur clean.

Claws

Retractable claws
Cats normally have their curved claws hidden away, which helps keep them sharp. When they want to use them – to do anything from climbing to hunting, fighting and scratching to leave scent marks – cats flex the tendons in their paws.

SHORTHAIR
Chausie

CHARACTERISTICS

Coat
Black and ticked tabby pattern in brown and grizzled black
Weight
3.6–7.3kg (8–16lb)
Lifespan
12–18 years
Personality
Intelligent, playful, affectionate
Origin
United States

An exotic-looking breed, the Chausie is a hybrid of domestic cats and the wild jungle cat, or *Felix chaus* – from which its name is derived. Although such hybrids have naturally existed for centuries, the Chausie was intentionally created in the 1990s, in part to provide an ethical alternative to keeping wild cats as house pets. In the early days, breeders crossed the jungle cat with many different domestic cats but, as time passed, only certain short-haired cats like the Abyssinian and Oriental Shorthair were used. Today, the svelte Chausie resembles its wild cat ancestor but has a friendly, affectionate demeanour. In fact, it enjoys the company of others so much that it hates being left alone and needs plenty of attention. This cat is extremely active, playful and intelligent, and can learn new tricks like playing fetch or walking on a lead. A Chausie is known to open cupboards and remove the contents on its own, too – it is not unheard of for owners to child-proof the house! Quite a handful, these fun-loving cats are more suited to experienced owners.

ABOVE:
Hybrid
The first recorded breeding of domestic and jungle cats was the hybrid Chausie, which gained full recognition by TICA in 2013.

ABOVE:
High jumper
Chausies are built for running and jumping. In fact, they can jump as much as 1.8m (6ft) straight up in the air!

OPPOSITE:
High energy
This breed is a long, lean and agile cat with bounds of energy that needs plenty of exercise.

ABOVE:
Friendly face
A Chausie cat can be trained to learn tricks and loves dedicated attention from its owner.

SHORTHAIR

ABOVE:
Greyhound cat
Cornish Rex cats – sometimes referred to as the Greyhound of cats with their long legs and tucked-up waistline – are very fast runners.

Cornish Rex

CHARACTERISTICS

Coat
Wavy or curly; all colours and patterns
Weight
2.3–4.5kg (5–10lb)
Lifespan
16+ years
Personality
Sociable, playful, affectionate
Origin
United Kingdom

This striking cat with a curly, or *rexed*, coat is the result of a natural mutation which occurred in the United Kingdom. In 1950, an unusual male kitten was born with curly fur and whiskers in an otherwise normal litter on a Cornish farm. It was this kitten, named Kallibunker, who became the founder of the Cornish Rex. Kallibunker and his descendants were bred to other cats – including the Siamese, Russian Blue and British Shorthair – to widen the genetic pool and develop the breed further.

A Cornish Rex has distinctive large ears and a long, slender body with a short, dense curly, wavy or rippled coat. Even its whiskers and eyebrows are curled or crinkled. Despite its elegant appearance, the energetic and playful Cornish Rex can be entertaining with its acrobatic and silly antics. It can even use its paws like little hands to open doors or cupboards – especially when bored – due to its long toes. This attention-seeking cat is always ready to play but also adores a warm lap at the end of the day.

ABOVE:
Unique traits
A Cornish Rex is noted for many unique traits, such as its short curly coat and oversized ears with prominent eyes and cheekbones.

SHORTHAIR

SHORTHAIR

LEFT:
Curls
Though Cornish Rex cats have a curly or wavy coat, kittens can temporarily lose their curls for a few weeks.

OPPOSITE TOP:
Young Rex
This playful, curious and energetic kitten remains the same as an adult and generally enjoys company – some even like to play fetch. Its big ears are thanks to the Siamese in its genes.

OPPOSITE BOTTOM:
Fine coat
This cat has a short, extremely fine, curly coat which means it cannot tolerate the cold and should mainly be kept indoors.

SHORTHAIR

Devon Rex

Due to a natural mutation, an adopted stray male kitten was born with a curly coat in 1960, in an abandoned tin mine in Devon. At first, this kitten – named Kirlee – was thought to be the curly-coated Cornish Rex that was discovered a few years earlier. However, it turned out that the gene responsible for the well-defined waves of the Cornish Rex coats was different to Kirlee's and a new breed was developed: the Devon Rex. This breed typically has missing or stubby whiskers and the curls on its coat are often tighter than those of a Cornish Rex. Also, the massive, low-set ears and big eyes are said to give the Devon Rex an almost pixie-like appearance. Aside from its attractive looks, the Devon Rex is a perfect companion for high-energy owners who generally stay at home. This charmful yet mischievous cat thrives around its family and wants to get involved in everything. As a powerful jumper, no spot goes unexplored and can often be found perched on your shoulder or lap, enjoying its velvety soft, wavy coat being petted.

CHARACTERISTICS

Coat
Wavy or curly; all colours and patterns
Weight
2.7–4.1kg (6–9lb)
Lifespan
12–16 years
Personality
Friendly, intelligent, playful, affectionate
Origin
United Kingdom

ABOVE:
Varying coat
A Devon Rex's curls often vary throughout its life, especially as a kitten.

RIGHT:
Short whiskers
This unusual-looking cat has crinkled, short whiskers because they tend to easily break off before reaching full length.

ABOVE:
Alien look-a-like
With huge ears, big eyes and a triangular face, the Devon Rex is often described as resembling gremlins or a relative of Star Wars' Yoda.

RIGHT:
High spots
Active and playful, the Devon Rex can often be found jumping up or climbing to high places and exploring them.

SHORTHAIR

BOTH PHOTOGRAPHS:
Pixie cats
As a kitten, the Devon Rex sheds and grows back its coat before the curly coat is fully formed in adulthood.

Donskoy

Also known as the Don Sphynx or Russian Hairless, this wrinkled, hairless cat with large ears and almond-shaped eyes originated in Russia in the late 1980s. Donskoy cats are descendants of a rescue kitten named Varvara, which was found in the streets of Rostov-on-Don and gradually became hairless due to a genetic mutation. While some Donskoy cats are indeed hairless, others have partial fuzzy or wavy coats. In fact, they can have four distinct coat types: the completely Rubber Bald; the chamois-like Flock Coat that can eventually disappear; the wavy, Velour coat where cats have a bald spot on top of their heads and the hair usually disappears everywhere except possibly some fuzz on the face, legs and tail; and the bristly, wavy Brush coat that always remains but cats may have some bald spots. Some Donskoy cats can also grow patches of fur in the winter and shed it once the seasons change. Like other hairless cats, the Donskoy requires regular bathing to get rid of oils from the skin.

CHARACTERISTICS

Coat
Hairless (or Rubber Bald), Flock, Velour or Brush; all colours and patterns
Weight
3.6–6.8kg (8–15lb)
Lifespan
12–15 years
Personality
Affectionate, gentle, sociable
Origin
Russia

LEFT:
Hairlessness
Due to a unique genetic mutation, some kittens are born completely hairless while others lose their hair over time.

ABOVE:
Companionship
This breed is known for being active and very sociable.

SHORTHAIR

Donskoy
This pear-shaped-bodied cat loves human companionship and can learn commands.

SHORTHAIR
Dragon Li

CHARACTERISTICS

Coat
Brown mackerel tabby pattern
Weight
4.1–5.4kg (9–12lb)
Lifespan
12–15 years
Personality
Active, friendly, intelligent
Origin
China

This brown mackerel tabby with yellow-green eyes, also known as the Chinese Li Hua, originated from domesticated cats in China called lí huā māo which translates to 'fox flower cat'. It is believed that these cats are descendants of a wild cat species, the Chinese mountain cat (*Felis bieti*) that domesticated itself over time, though this theory is somewhat controversial because the African wildcat (*Felis lybica*) is known to be the ancestor of the domestic cat. The derived standardized breed is recognized by China's Cat Aficionado Association (CAA). It was also recognized as an experimental breed by the US-based, international Cat Fanciers' Association (CFA) in 2003 but this was later revoked. The Dragon Li is a medium-sized, muscular cat that has ticked hairs that form a beautiful mackerel tabby pattern – a pattern with vertical stripes instead of swirls. Not particularly fond of cuddling or being confined in an apartment, this loyal companion prefers to be in places with plenty of space to exercise or to use its extraordinary hunting skills.

ABOVE:
Mackerel tabby
This wild-looking cat has long, narrow vertical stripes across its body that resemble a fish skeleton, known as a mackerel pattern.

ABOVE:
Chinese breed
The Dragon Li is unofficially considered the national cat of China and is rarely seen outside its origin country.

SHORTHAIR

ABOVE:
Dragon Li
In Chinese folklore, dragons are a symbol of power, strength and good luck, hence its name.

RIGHT:
Running wild
This precious Chinese tabby kitten will become a large, muscular cat that will need space in which to keep active.

SHORTHAIR

Egyptian Mau

This graceful, rare cat, with gooseberry-green eyes, is the only natural domesticated breed of spotted cat, thought to have originated in Ancient Egypt where cats held a special place. Though difficult to trace direct descent, art depictions that resemble the Egyptian Mau can be seen on ancient temples and tombs and some cats were even mummified. During the Roman rule of Egypt, Romans likely brought back to Italy some of these spotted cats with distinctive mascara and barring face markings. The Egyptian Mau we know today was developed in the 1950s in the United States, after WW2, imported from Italy. While historical evidence suggests that the breed is Egyptian, genetic studies have revealed that this modern Egyptian Mau is now mostly of European and North American origin, and more closely related to breeds like the Maine Coon. Known for their quality companionship and hunting prowess, Egyptian Maus are said to make very loyal and loving pets.

CHARACTERISTICS

Coat
Spotted pattern in silver, bronze and black smoke
Weight
2.7–6.4kg (6–14lbs)
Lifespan
12–15 years
Personality
Active, loyal, affectionate
Origin
Egypt

ABOVE:
Smell
A cat's nose is much better than ours at picking up scents. Smell helps cats identify people, objects, other cats or animals, as well as track their prey.

RIGHT
Fastest cat
The Egyptian Mau holds the record for the fastest domestic cat, reaching speeds of up to 48km/h (30mph).

SHORTHAIR

OPPOSITE:
Devoted companion
Egyptian Maus are playful, affectionate and loyal to their owners but generally do not take to strangers.

ABOVE TOP:
Typical marks
An Egyptian Mau's spots appear on the tips of its hairs and its forehead is marked with the letter 'M'.

ABOVE BOTTOM:
Bags of energy
This high-energy breed has powerful legs that make it an excellent runner and leaper and requires frequent exercise.

SHORTHAIR

ABOVE:
Colourful coats
Dark brown is the original colour for Burmese cats but they now take on a range of hues.

European Burmese

CHARACTERISTICS

Coat
10 solid and tortie colours, including brown, chocolate and lilac

Weight
2.7–6.4 kg (6–14lb)

Lifespan
Up to 18 years

Personality
Social, playful, vocal

Origin
Burma (Myanmar) / United Kingdom

Similar to the American Burmese, this breed originated in Myanmar (formerly Burma). However, it is the result of breeding programmes in the United Kingdom, in the 1950s, involving Burmese cats of various builds brought over from the United States. The European and American varieties were originally considered to be genetically distinct. The European Burmese, then called British Burmese, was officially recognised in 1952 by the Governing Council of the Cat Fancy (GCCF) in the UK. However, the European Burmese – also known as traditional Burmese – was no longer considered a separate breed by the Cat Fanciers' Association (CFA) in the 1980s.

In addition, most cat registries do not formally recognise these as separate breeds, though they use these separate breed standards. The European Burmese distinguishes itself from its American relative due to its thinner build and head, more slender ears, eyes that are more almond-shaped rather than round, and longer legs and muzzle. Both varieties are medium-sized and often feel heavy due to their muscular build.

ABOVE:
Active companions
European Burmese cats are known to be playful, even as adults, and enjoy the company of humans.

SHORTHAIR

European Shorthair

Resembling the typical domestic cats of Europe, this breed was developed in Sweden in the 1980s from ordinary domestic cats. Confusingly, the stockier British Shorthair was also called European Shorthair at that time, even though they had distinct traits. What's more, these were judged by the same breed standards until 1981 when the International Feline Federation (FIFe) registered the European as a separate breed. Also called the Celtic Shorthair, the European Shorthair is a skilled mouse-hunter that will clear its surroundings of rodents, whether it is kept indoors or outdoors. It tends to adapt easily to changes and can happily live in an active home, along with children or other pets. However, cats of this breed can also be shy around strangers and may seek out a safe place to hide. Known to be quite active and playful, European Shorthairs also enjoy taking naps anywhere and will also make themselves comfortable on a warm lap.

CHARACTERISTICS

Coat
Various colours and patterns
Weight
3.6–6.8kg (8–15lb)
Lifespan
15–20 years
Personality
Active, friendly, intelligent
Origin
Sweden

ABOVE:
Widely wanted
The European Shorthair is a popular breed in Scandinavia and Germany.

RIGHT:
Even-tempered
This breed is physically very supple and strong and is often chosen for being even-tempered.

SHORTHAIR

Natural hunters
European Shorthairs thrive indoors and outdoors – and both places will undoubtedly be cleared of rodents!

SHORTHAIR

OPPOSITE
Low maintenance
This calm and reserved breed is excellent for first-time owners due to its low-maintenance personality and easy grooming requirements.

ABOVE TOP:
Lookout
In any outdoor garden setting, this cat will be on the lookout for prey and challenges from any local feline neighbours.

ABOVE BOTTOM:
European domestic cats
European shorthair is sometimes used as an umbrella term for common domestic cats of Europe, which causes some confusion.

SHORTHAIR

Exotic Shorthair

This cuddly, gentle breed was developed in the 1960s. It came about when breeders wanted to create a short-haired version of the Persian by crossing it with the American Shorthair. It got its name from the colour of its coat, which was initially greyish-silver and was considered to be an exotic hue. In some breed registries, Exotic Shorthairs are classified as a separate breed, while in others they are considered to be a short-haired variety of the Persian.

American Shorthairs look a lot like Persians since they are relatives. They both have a round head, flat face, full cheeks and large, round eyes. Although the Exotic Shorthair's fur is shorter, its coat is made up of two layers and is plush. It doesn't shed much and typically needs to be combed once a week. The Exotic Shorthair is livelier than its long-haired cousin, which is often described as lazy or 'furniture with fur'. However, it is pudgy in appearance due to its dense bones. Like Persians, Exotic Shorthairs enjoy attention and like having someone around to play with or cuddle.

CHARACTERISTICS

Coat
Most colours and patterns
Weight
3.6–6.8 kg (8–15 pounds)
Lifespan
12–15 years
Personality
Quiet, gentle, easy-going, affectionate
Origin
United States

LEFT:
Breed of its own
The Exotic Shorthair was first recognized as its own breed in 1967 by the Cat Fanciers' Association (CFA).

ABOVE:
Quirks
Short-nosed breeds, such as the Exotic Shorthair, often stick out their tongue for long periods of time.

SHORTHAIR

ABOVE:
Grumpy cat
This laid-back cat unsurprisingly looks a lot like its relative, the Persian breed, but with a shorter coat.

OPPOSITE:
Young exotic shorthair
The exotic shorthair is a crossbreed of a Persian and various short-haired breeds, including the American shorthair.

SHORTHAIR
German Rex

CHARACTERISTICS

Coat
Wavy or curly; all colours and patterns
Weight
2.7–4.5kg (6–10lb)
Lifespan
12–15 years
Personality
Intelligent, playful, affectionate
Origin
Germany

As the name suggests, this rare breed was developed in Germany. The ancestor of the German Rex was a black curly-coated stray female named Lämmchen. She was found wandering in a garden outside a hospital in Berlin in the late 1940s. Her name is derived from the German for 'young lamb', alluding to the way the curly coat made her look. Not only did her descendants make up the new breed, but it is said that they were also used to refine other breeds such as the Cornish Rex. Friendly and loving, German Rex cats quickly form bonds with their family. They welcome all the attention they can get and love their velvety, curly coat to be stroked – especially after burning off their boundless energy and playfulness with fun games. Despite the short coat, these cats still need to be regularly groomed and bathed. Since 1982, the International Feline Federation (FIFe) is the only major breed organization that recognizes the German Rex.

ABOVE:
Same mutation
This intelligent breed from Germany has curly fur and whiskers due to the same genetic mutation found in the Cornish Rex.

SHORTHAIR

ABOVE:
Soft velvet
The German Rex does not have an outer layer of fur, or *guard hairs*.
This makes its short, wavy coat feel like soft velvet.

SHORTHAIR

Big ears
This charming German Rex kitten has distinctive large ears which appear too big for its head!

SHORTHAIR

SHORTHAIR

LEFT:
Curly whiskers
This breed's whiskers curl, though less strongly than those of the Cornish Rex. They may also be nearly straight.

ABOVE:
Long legs
Very long, slender legs make German Rex cats appear larger than they are – but are usually bigger than the Cornish Rex.

SHORTHAIR
Havana

With dazzling green eyes and brown whiskers, this extremely rare breed has a very confusing history. In the United Kingdom, breeders developed a rich brown cat, known as Havana, in the early 1950s, using Siamese and domestic shorthairs. In 1958, the Governing Council of the Cat Fancy (GCCF) recognized this new breed as the Chestnut Foreign Shorthair, which later changed to Havana and is now known as a solid-coloured Oriental Shorthair. Meanwhile, in the mid-1950s, the first Havana cats arrived in the United States to create the Havana Brown – the Havana we know today.

Since North American breeders did not use the Siamese, this cat has a rounder face and a less elongated body than the English Havanas. Its strikingly gorgeous looks are hard to ignore, though the affectionate Havana will not complain about the extra attention – on the contrary, it seeks and asks for it. It also likes to be involved in every activity in the household and usually has the very last word. Today, the Cat Fanciers' Association (CFA) and the Canadian Cat Association (CCA-AFC) both recognize the breed as Havana Brown, while it is known as Havana by The International Cat Association (TICA).

CHARACTERISTICS

Coat
Rich brown (towards mahogany) or lilac
Weight
2.7–4.5kg (6–10lb)
Lifespan
8–15 years
Personality
Curious, playful, intelligent
Origin
United Kingdom / United States

ABOVE:
Rich brown
Noted for its rich chocolate-brown coat, it is said that the Havana got its name from the Havana cigar.

RIGHT
Havanas
Chocolate-brown Orientals are confusingly called Havanas in the UK but these cats have a wedge-shaped face and elongated bodies, resembling the Siamese.

OPPOSITE:
Close resemblance
Often confused with the North American breed, this captivating chocolate-brown cat is in fact an Oriental Shorthair.

ABOVE:
Matching
Havana cats have mesmerising, oval green eyes, and noses and whiskers that match their rich brown coat colour.

SHORTHAIR

ABOVE:
Fun-loving
A Highlander's unique appearance, with its loosely curled ears and short tail, and fun-loving personality will steal your heart.

Highlander

CHARACTERISTICS

Coat
All colours in tabby pattern, including colourpoints
Weight
4.5–9.1kg (10–20lb)
Lifespan
10–15 years
Personality
Affectionate, gentle, playful, energetic
Origin
United States

Formerly known as the Highlander Lynx, this wild-looking cat has distinctive curled ears, a big, muscular body and a short tail. Its ears, in particular, have a loose curl on the top third of the ear, while its naturally stubby short tail can have kinks and curls in it. The Highlander, which also comes in a long-haired version, was developed in 2004 from crossing two experimental cats, the Desert Lynx and the Jungle Curl. Though Highlander cats have a wild look and their long back legs make them look like they are ready to pounce, these large cats are gentle and loving of everyone. In fact, they thrive on attention and affection, and cannot get enough of playing, especially games of chase. They are even said to wag their short tails when happy and playing. The Highlander is still very rare but makes a devoted and lively companion in any home.

ABOVE:
Tails
The Highlander has a naturally short tail that ranges from about 2.5 to 15cm (1 to 6in) long, though some cats are born with full-length tails.

SHORTHAIR

FAR RIGHT:
Loyal companion
This people-oriented cat is friendly with almost anyone, including strangers, but loves its family the most.

RIGHT TOP AND BOTTOM:
Characteristics
This heavyweight, rare cat is noted for its curled ears, tabby markings and bobbed tail.

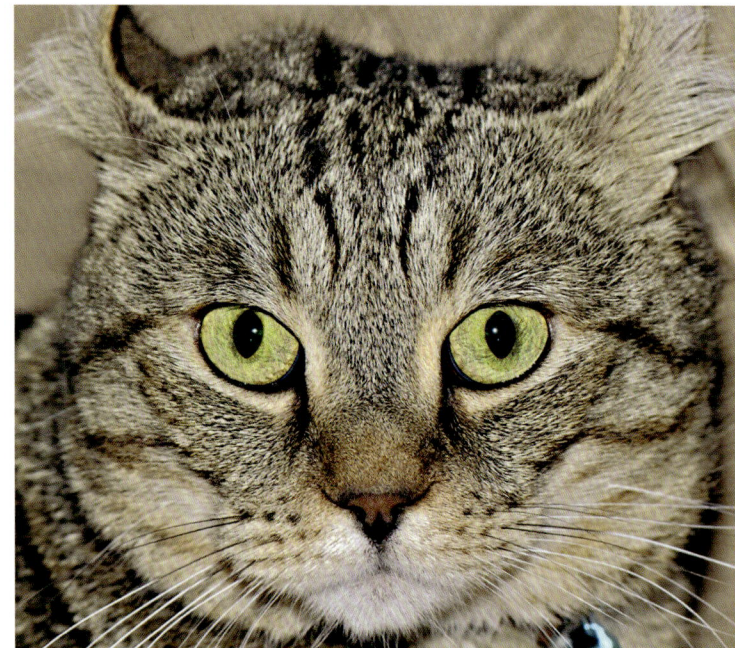

SHORTHAIR
Japanese Bobtail

As the name suggests, this ancient cat from Japan has a very short, or bobbed, tail, often called a 'pom-pom'. It is said that its tail more closely resembles that of a rabbit than any other bobtailed cat. Japanese Bobtails – both long-haired and short-haired – appear to have been favoured pets in Japan for several hundred years. However, their exact origin remains a mystery. Many experts argue that this cat originated in Southeast Asia or southern China at least a thousand years ago before it was brought to the island. In fact, recent research has found that short-tailed feral domestic cats in those areas have the same mutation that causes the short tails in Japanese Bobtails. Some believe that they were first introduced by Buddhist monks in the 6th century who used them to protect rice paper scrolls from rodents. Japanese folklore even suggests that all cats' tails were shortened on the emperor's orders because one lost its tail in a fire while sleeping! Regardless, these charming, outgoing and affectionate cats enjoy spending time with their owners, playing or chatting – even singing – while they sit next to them.

CHARACTERISTICS
Coat
Short or long; all colours and patterns
Weight
2.7–4.5kg (6–10lb)
Lifespan
9–15 years
Personality
Active, intelligent, outgoing, affectionate
Origin
Japan

ABOVE:
Tail shape
Due to a natural genetic mutation, this breed's unique tail can be straight, curved or kinked.

RIGHT:
Lucky breed
Traditionally found in Japanese folklore and art, it is said that Japanese Bobtails bring good luck.

SHORTHAIR

ABOVE TOP AND BOTTOM:
Happy kitties
These cats are good-natured and playful, making them ideal house pets.

RIGHT:
Bobtails
The tails on the Japanese Bobtails are all distinct – no two are alike!

Kanaani

With a long, slender, muscular body and large tufted ears, this rare cat is a crossbreed of short-haired cats and spotted African wildcats (*Felis lybica*). It was developed in the 1990s in Jerusalem, Israel, and is said to take its name from the historical settlement of 'Canaan'. Although the Kanaani was recognized by the World Cat Federation (WCF) in 2000, no other cat registry accepts it as a breed. Very few breeding programmes exist only in Germany and the United States. The Kanaani could be crossed with spotted African wildcats and spotted Oriental Shorthairs or Bengal cats but has been allowed to only have Kanaani parents since 2008. Active and playful, the Kanaani loves to jump and climb in high places. Its inner wild makes this breed an excellent hunter and quite independent so it requires plenty of space. However, Kanaani cats are also very affectionate and enjoy time with their family – though make ideal pets for households with older children.

LEFT:
Wild spots
The Kanaani was developed to look wild and resemble spotted African wildcats. However, it now comes in a marbled tabby pattern too.

ABOVE:
Identifiable features
Except for its spotted or marbled coat, this breed has a distinctive big triangular-shaped head and large, almond-shaped green eyes.

CHARACTERISTICS

Coat
Various colours in spotted and marbled tabby patterns
Weight
4.1–8.2kg (9–18lb)
Lifespan
12–15 years
Personality
Playful, athletic, intelligent, affectionate
Origin
Israel

SHORTHAIR

ABOVE:
Active kittens
These lively kittens get their looks and energy from their African wildcat ancestors.

RIGHT AND OPPOSITE:
Elegance
This athletic yet elegant breed has large ears and a long, spotted body.

SHORTHAIR
Khao Manee

CHARACTERISTICS

Coat
White
Weight
2.7–5kg (6–11lb)
Lifespan
10–12 years
Personality
Playful, outgoing, curious
Origin
Thailand

One of the rarest cat breeds, the white-coated Khao Manee is also known as the Diamond Eye cat because of its brilliant, colourful gemstone-like eyes. These can be blue, green, gold, odd-coloured or even have multiple colours within one eye. Its name means 'white jewel' in its native country of Thailand, where it developed naturally hundreds of years ago. Like the Siamese, Thai, Suphalak and Korat, the Khao Manee is mentioned in a book of poems about cats from the 14th century, said to bring good fortune. The Khao Manee was previously kept only by Thai royalty and is still relatively rare in the West, first being imported to the United States in 1999. In 2015, The International Cat Association (TICA) was the first breed organization to fully recognize the Khao Manee. Graceful and devoted, Khao Manee cats make wonderful companions. They are curious and love to explore and play – even get into some mischief – before cuddling up on laps for a warm nap.

ABOVE:
Distinctive traits
The Khao Manee has a distinctive heart-shaped head, high cheekbones and jewel-like eyes that can be odd-coloured.

ABOVE:
Good luck cat
Odd-eyed Khao Manee cats are the rarest variety and are favoured because they are thought to be lucky.

Eyes

Vision

PREVIOUS PAGES:
Cat vision
Cats are better adapted to seeing in low light – when they are usually more active – but they can also see colours. They can distinguish blues and yellows, whereas reds and greens can look grey or be confusing. Cat vision isn't as sharp as ours and so cats mostly rely on detecting movement.

ABOVE:
Night vision
In the dark, cats can see six to eight times better than us, thanks to the many light receptors in their eyes called rods and a mirror-like structure in the back of the eye called the tapetum lucidum. The tapetum reflects any uncaught light that passes through the eye – this is what makes cats' eyes glow at night.

RIGHT:
Pupil shape
Viewed up close, a cat's eye has vertical slit pupils. Though it makes cats look terrifying, this allows them to see in bright daylight by limiting how much light enters their eyes. Conversely, in low light, the pupils expand – three times more than ours – to allow in additional light, and cover most of the eye.

SHORTHAIR
Korat

Named for a Thai province, the Korat is an ancient breed from Phimai in Thailand, dating back to at least the 14th century. It is believed that the Korat was first introduced to Europe in the 1890s as a 'blue Siamese' due to its Siamese-like appearance yet with a blue-grey coat and large, radiant green eyes. Unlike many other cat breeds, Korat cats still closely resemble their ancestors without having been crossed to any other breed. Even breed standards have not changed over time. In fact, often referred to as the 'silver-blue cat with the Thai passport', all Korat cats in the West can have their ancestry traced back to imports from Thailand. This charming cat makes a fun and quite demanding companion. An attention-seeker, the Korat considers itself in charge of its family and will demand interactive play and companionship. However, it will also often climb on laps or arms to show its gentle affection and get some in return.

CHARACTERISTICS
Coat
Only blue with silver tips
Weight
2.7–4.5kg (6–10lb)
Lifespan
15+ years
Personality
Intelligent, affectionate, demanding
Origin
Thailand

ABOVE:
Good fortune
In its homeland, the Korat is considered good fortune and a pair of these cats is gifted to newlyweds or highly respected individuals.

RIGHT
Luminous eyes
Korats are known for their distinctive blue coats, heart-shaped heads and large, round, green eyes. Young cats' eyes gradually change from amber to green.

SHORTHAIR

ABOVE:
Cuddles
This cat has a wild streak but is also very affectionate and sweet-tempered.

Kurilian Bobtail

CHARACTERISTICS

Coat
Most solid colours; bicolour, tortie and tabby patterns
Weight
3.6–6.8kg (8–15lb)
Lifespan
15–20 years
Personality
Gentle, sociable, intelligent
Origin
Kuril Islands, Sakhalin Island, Kamchatka peninsula

Named after the Kuril Islands in the North Pacific, the Kurilian Bobtail originated from these islands, as well as the Sakhalin Island and the Kamchatka peninsula of Russia. Its distinctive short, kinked tail is a natural mutation that occurred at least 200 years ago. Both Russia and Japan have claimed the Kuril Islands so it is unclear which countries the Kurilian Bobtail comes from. This stocky breed – both short-haired and long-haired – is a skilled hunter and excellent fish catcher, but is also gentle and affectionate and loves family life. It adapts well to children and other animals, and after its daily exercise or play session, it enjoys a good cuddle with its owners – it even loves to sleep in the same bed! So as long as it is in company and has places to climb, perch and play, the captivating, wild-looking Kurilian Bobtail is happy in any loving household.

ABOVE:
Pom-pom tail
Kurilian Bobtails are known for their wild appearance and pom-pom-like tails.

Unique direction
Tails of a Kurilian Bobtail are never the same – between two and ten vertebrae, they can kink or curve in any direction!

SHORTHAIR
LaPerm

With a wavy or curly coat, the LaPerm originated with a cat named Curly. In 1982, a brown tabby barn cat in Oregon gave birth to a litter of six kittens, one of which was completely bald. After about eight weeks, this kitten started to grow soft, wavy fur, and that was the start of the breed. LaPerm cats have a soft, springy coat that can be either short or long, though the short-haired coat can feel a little harder, standing out from the body with waves, and the tail looks like a bottlebrush. They tend to get deeply attached to their family in a household with or without children, or other pets.

Though happy with the attention and affection, especially while sitting in laps, the LaPerm is very active and needs high amounts of exercise and play. In fact, it loves to climb and jump, and a good game of fetch or chase, before cuddling up and purring softly on a lap.

CHARACTERISTICS
Coat
All colours and patterns
Weight
2.7–5.4kg (6–12lb)
Lifespan
12–15 years
Personality
Active, affectionate, intelligent
Origin
United States

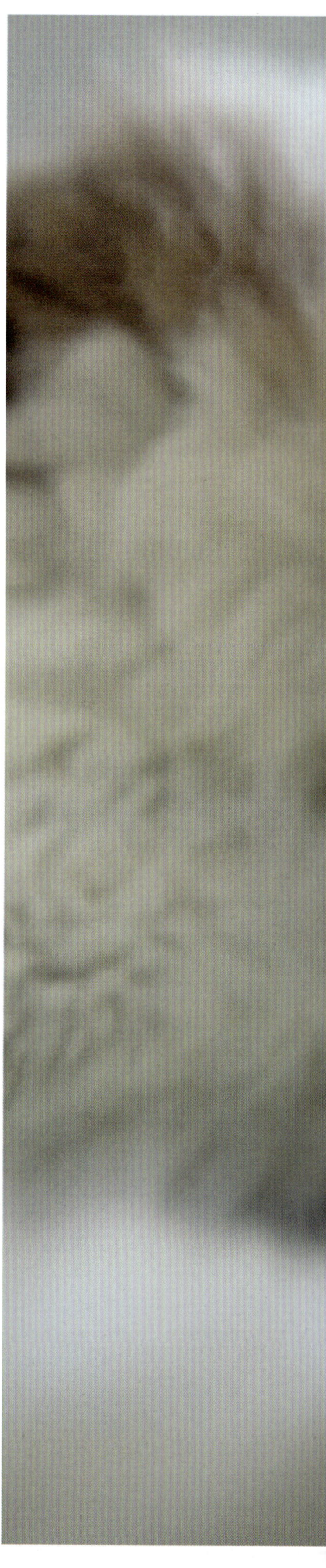

ABOVE:
Natural mutation
This rex-coated breed, with long curly whiskers, is named after its wavy or curly coat that was discovered in the 1980s – thanks to a natural mutation.

RIGHT:
Springy
The light, springy coat of the LaPerm stands away from the body, which makes the cat look rather fluffy.

SHORTHAIR

ABOVE:
Curly kitten
This kitten with very long curly whiskers looks like it has had a shaggy perm.

OPPOSITE:
Lambswool
The coat of the short-haired cat has a more textured feel, just like lambswool.

SHORTHAIR

Lykoi

Resembling a werewolf with its wiry look and thin – often black-grey – fur, this cat is unsurprisingly nicknamed *werewolf cat* and *wolf cat*. In fact, Lykoi cats get their name from the Greek word for 'wolves'. They can be covered entirely in hair, looking more like an opossum, or be partially hairless which gives them a more wolfish appearance. Sometimes they even lose all of their hair but it grows back. Their look is the result of a natural mutation that was discovered in feral domestic cats in the early 2010s in the United States. However, records show that these unusual-looking feral cats existed well over 40 years ago. Wolf-like looks aside, the Lykoi makes an excellent pet. Outgoing and friendly, it can get along with anyone and loves every member of its family – human or animal. It is particularly fond of play and, with its strong prey drive, it can often be found stalking and pouncing on its toys or family. However, it is best to keep Lykoi cats indoors because their sparse hair makes them prone to sunburn and skin damage.

CHARACTERISTICS

Coat
Partially hairless; all colours in roan pattern
Weight
2.7–5.4kg (6–12lb)
Lifespan
12–15 years
Personality
Outgoing, friendly, playful
Origin
United States

LEFT:
Werewolf
This cat has a hairless mask that connects its muzzle, eyes and ears, which makes it appear like a werewolf.

ABOVE:
Roan pattern
The Lykoi has a unique colour pattern on its coat called *roan*, which consists of scattered white hairs throughout its body.

SHORTHAIR

SHORTHAIR

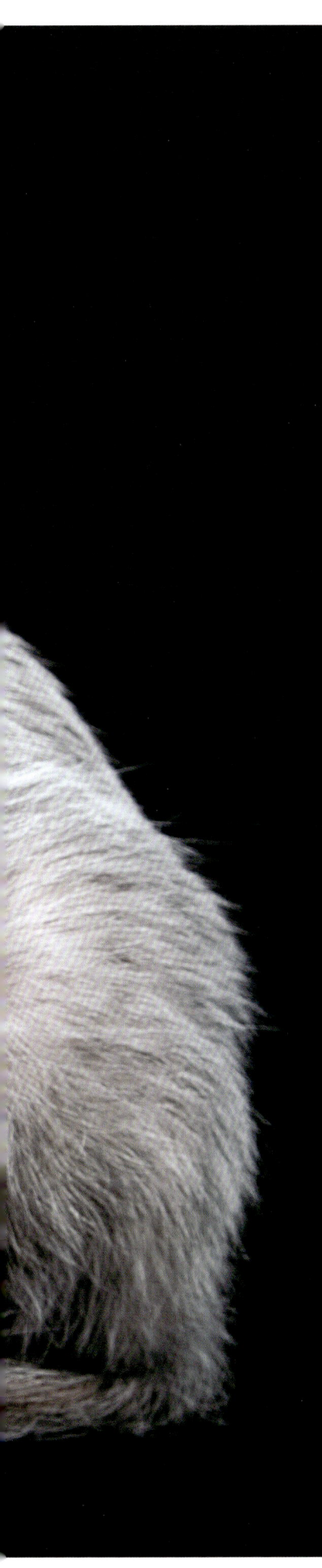

LEFT:
Crouching Lykoi
The unusual look of this breed is due to a natural mutation of a domestic shorthair.

ABOVE:
Unusual looks
Despite its unusual werewolf-like looks, the Lykoi is also known for its loyal dog-like behaviour.

SHORTHAIR
Mandalay

CHARACTERISTICS

Coat
Many colours and patterns
Weight
2.7–6.4kg (6–14lb)
Lifespan
Up to 18 years
Personality
Active, playful, affectionate
Origin
New Zealand

Originating in New Zealand from accidental matings, this breed is essentially a Burmese in a greater variety of coats and eye colours. In the early 1970s, on the South Island, a cream Burmese mated with a red domestic shorthair, which resulted in rich reddish-brown kittens. Meanwhile on the North Island, jet-black kittens with amber eyes were born to a seal Burmese and a black domestic shorthair in the late 1980s. From both these stunning litters, the two breeders went on to develop a new breed: the Mandalay. As time passed, Abyssinians were also used to introduce cinnamon and fawn-coloured coats. Best known in New Zealand and Australia, Mandalay cats are said to resemble the short-haired Asian cats bred in Europe. Similar to the Burmese, these elegant cats are fun-loving and playful, and happiest in an active household. When the Mandalay isn't playing, it likes to follow its owners around or cuddle up in their lap.

ABOVE:
Rich colour
Even when the Mandalay has the same coat colour as the Burmese, the Mandalay's is more intense and uniform throughout its head and body.

ABOVE:
Vocally expressive
Like the Burmese, the Mandalay isn't shy about letting you know when it needs your attention. Its voice can sound like a crying baby!

SHORTHAIR
Manx

There are many tales about how the tailless cat of the Isle of Man, known as Manx, came to be. It is said that a tailless cat swam to the island after a shipwreck of the Spanish Armada, or that the cat lost its tail on Noah's Ark because, arriving late, it got slammed in the door. Some even say it is a "cabbit", a mixture of a cat and a rabbit! In actual fact, its lack of tail is a natural mutation – and as well as non-existent tails, Manx cats can also have partial or full tails. However, taillessness sometimes comes with spinal issues but these are now rare due to carefully controlled breeding.

The Manx is one of the oldest breeds and has been around from at least the 18th century. Noted for their impeccable hunting skills, Manx cats were traditionally kept by farmers or on ships to limit rodents. Today – together with their long-haired version known as Cymric – they are a popular pet for any family because of their attractive appearance and amiable temperament.

CHARACTERISTICS
Coat
Dense, in all colours and patterns
Weight
3.6–5.4kg (8–12lb)
Lifespan
14–16 years
Personality
Gentle, mellow, playful, sociable, intelligent
Origin
United Kingdom

ABOVE:
Tail length
Manx cats are classified according to their tail length: the entirely tailless *rumpy*; a short bump or *rumpy-riser*; the short-tailed *stumpy*; and *longie*, with an almost normal length tail.

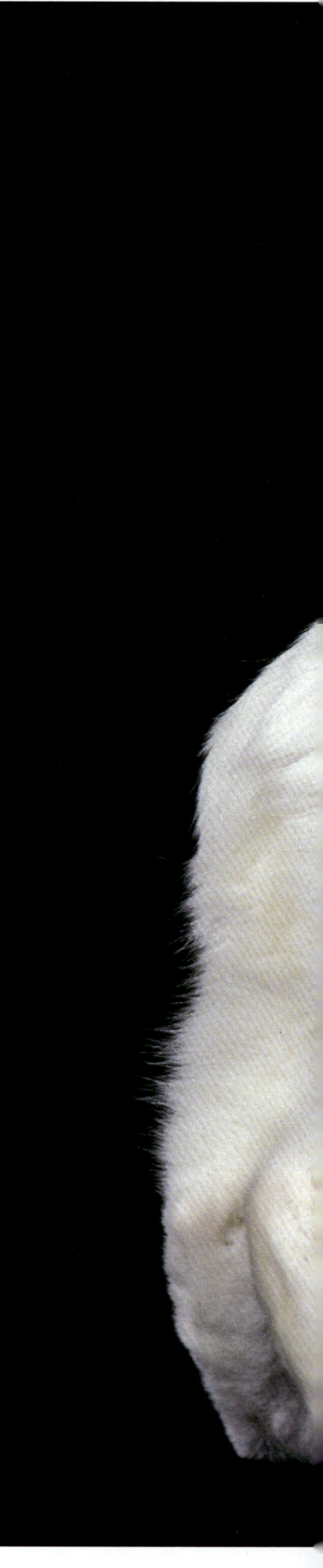

RIGHT
Rabbit-like shape
A Manx is rabbit-like, with its rounded rump, long back legs and stumpy tail.

SHORTHAIR

RIGHT:
Manx kitten
This breed is very sociable and playful by nature.

OPPOSITE:
Ready to pounce
The Manx's legs help it run extremely fast and jump extraordinarily high – as much as 1.2m (4ft) from standing position!

SHORTHAIR

ABOVE:
Short legs
Munchkin cats are adorable and beloved feline companions known for their unique short legs.

Munchkin

CHARACTERISTICS

Coat
All colours and patterns
Weight
2.3–4.1kg (5–9lb)
Lifespan
15–18 years
Personality
Affectionate, curious, playful, intelligent
Origin
United States

This rare breed, nicknamed *sausage cat*, has short legs – sometimes even almost half the average length of other cats. Munchkins owe these exceptionally short legs to a random mutation. Short-legged cats have occurred naturally around the world since the 1940s, but the first Munchkins were bred in Louisiana in the 1980s. Both short-haired and long-haired versions were officially recognized by The International Cat Association (TICA) in 2003. However, many other breed organizations have refused to accept this somewhat controversial breed. Despite this, the gene for short legs does not seem to affect their health or lifespan. Munchkins make loving family pets that lead full lives and delight owners with their playfulness and affectionate cuddles. These small cats may not be able to jump as high or far as the average cat, but they are very fast, active and love a good game with the family. In fact, Munchkins are known to take, hide and collect shiny objects, just like magpies – but this is a game usually played without your knowledge! Due to their popularity, Munchkins have also been used to create other short-legged breeds.

ABOVE:
Shortest cat
Munchkins are the shortest cat breed in the world.

SHORTHAIR

SHORTHAIR

OPPOSITE TOP AND BOTTOM:
Shortest cat
Munchkins are the shortest cat breed in the world. At only 13.3cm (5.25in) tall, Lilieput – a tortie Munchkin from California – holds the Guinness World Record for the shortest living domestic cat.

ABOVE:
On the move
This short-legged kitten is full of energy, runs quite fast and loves to play with the family. Munchkins can often have slightly longer back legs than front legs.

SHORTHAIR
Ocicat

The first Ocicat was a spotted kitten named Tonga, born by accident in Michigan in 1964 as an attempt to develop a Siamese with points similar to the Abyssinian's ticked coat. While Tonga was sold as a pet, other intentional matings eventually produced more spotted kittens that became the founders of this breed. These kittens were thought to resemble a wild ocelot (*Leopardus pardalis*) which led to the name Ocicat. As the Ocicat was further developed to mimic this wild look, the American Shorthair was included in the breeding programme, in addition to the Siamese and Abyssinian. Lithe and well-muscled, this athletic cat loves playing games but will also have a cuddle. It can be easily trained to play fetch, walk on a leash or even follow voice commands like dogs. A gregarious and lovely temperament makes these cats wonderful companions in bustling households. The Governing Council of the Cat Fancy (GCCF) in the UK also recognises the Ocicat Classic, which is essentially an Ocicat in a classic tabby coat.

CHARACTERISTICS

Coat
Various colours in spotted tabby pattern
Weight
2.7–6.4kg (6–14lb)
Lifespan
15–18 years
Personality
Active, sociable, playful
Origin
United States

ABOVE:
Spotted coat
Named for its resemblance to the wild ocelot, the stunning Ocicat has a short, spotted coat that is easy to care for.

RIGHT:
Face markings
This spotted cat has a distinguishable tabby 'M' pattern on its forehead and markings that resemble mascara are found around the eyes and cheeks.

SHORTHAIR

Ocelot lookalike
The ocicat has fascinating markings that give it a wild appearance even though it possesses no wild DNA.

SHORTHAIR
Oriental Shorthair

CHARACTERISTICS

Coat
Many colours; tabby, tortie and bicolour patterns

Weight
3.6–6.4kg (8–14lb)

Lifespan
12–15 years

Personality
Affectionate, curious, playful, sociable, vocal

Origin
United Kingdom

The name may suggest otherwise, but Oriental Shorthairs originated in the United Kingdom in the 1950s. After World War II, the number of many cat breeds had shrunk. To revive the Siamese, English breeders crossed them with other short-haired cats like the Russian Blue, British Shorthair and Abyssinian. The result was a Siamese in a wide range of coat colours and patterns, other than colourpoint. At first, each non-pointed hybrid was recognized as a separate breed: the all-white Foreign White, the rich dark brown Havana, and the Oriental Tabby. But breeders soon realized that there were too many possible colour combinations and different coat lengths, and thus all non-pointed cats became known as the Oriental Shorthairs and Longhairs.

Like its Siamese relative, the Oriental Shorthair is svelte and elegant with a vibrant personality. It is very chatty and not shy about demanding the almost constant attention it craves from its family members – be that humans or other animals. This lively cat makes a fun and devoted companion but is not for those who are not at home much or want to live a quiet life.

ABOVE:
Love of play
Playful and curious, this adorable Oriental Shorthair kitten will never grow out of its love of play – especially fetch – remaining kitten-like all its life.

ABOVE:
Foreign Shorthair
Oriental Shorthairs, also known as Foreign Shorthairs, look similar to the Siamese but come in many coat colours and patterns.

ABOVE:
Oriental kitten
This adorable kitten with almond-shaped eyes and bat-like ears comes with a strong personality.

RIGHT:
Oriental bicolour
With white always covering its muzzle, underside and legs, this svelte short-haired oriental bicolour was first developed in the United States in the 1970s. Only the GCCF recognizes the Oriental Bicolour as a separate breed.

LEFT:
Triangular shaped
All Oriental cats have the same wedge-shaped heads as the modern Siamese cats.

ABOVE:
Affection
This precious kitten, with large ears and almond-shaped eyes, loves to give affection and expects it in return.

SHORTHAIR
Peterbald

A graceful Russian breed, the Peterbald was intentionally created in St Petersburg in 1994 by crossing the Oriental Shorthair with the Donskoy. It resembles the Oriental Shorthair with its wedge-shaped head, almond-shaped eyes, large ears and slender, muscular body. From the Donskoy, it inherited the hair-losing gene which causes the Peterbald to be born hairless, or to have a very fine undercoat or a dense, stiff coat. Specifically, the Peterbald can have five distinct coat types: naked or completely hairless; peach-like fuzz called chamois; the fine to slightly dense, flock coat; the wiry or wavy brush coat; and a full, straight coat. Those born with hair – except for those with straight coats – can lose it over time. Regardless of how much hair or fuzz it has, the Peterbald is sweet-tempered, affectionate and exceptionally outgoing, making it a good family pet. But like other hairless breeds, the Peterbald is best kept indoors because its skin is sensitive to the cold and sunshine.

CHARACTERISTICS
Coat
Hairless (naked), flock, chamois, brush or straight; all colours and patterns
Weight
3.6–6.8kg (8–15lb)
Lifespan
12–15 years
Personality
Affectionate, intelligent, outgoing
Origin
Russia

ABOVE:
Full coat
The Peterbald's coat can change several times over the first few years of life and it may lose or grow hair repeatedly.

RIGHT
Healthy appetite
Hairless or very thin-coated Peterbald cats have a faster metabolism than full-coated cats. This means they have healthy appetites!

SHORTHAIR

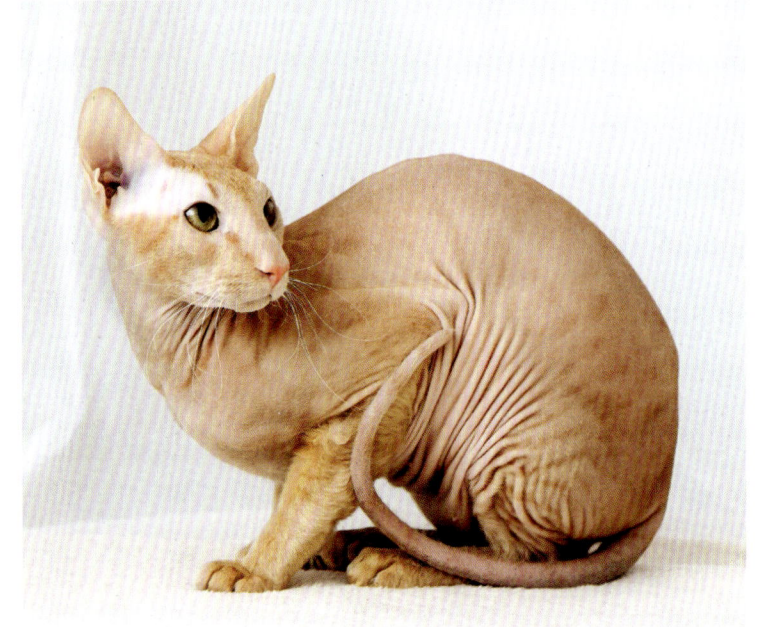

ALL PHOTOGRAPHS:
Fast metabolism
Due to the lack of fur, this charming breed has a faster metabolism than cats with full coats, which means it has a healthier appetite and heals more quickly from scratches or wounds.

SHORTHAIR

ABOVE:
Vocalization
Most Pixiebobs do not meow; instead, they prefer to chirp, chatter and occasionally growl to communicate with their humans.

Pixiebob

CHARACTERISTICS

Coat
Short or long, brown-spotted tabby
Weight
3.6–7.7kg (8–17lb)
Lifespan
12–15 years
Personality
Easy-going, affectionate, sociable
Origin
United States

Resembling the North American bobcat, this entirely domestic large cat has a thick brown-spotted coat, tufted ears and a bobbed tail. Both short and long-haired versions were developed in the late 1980s to deliberately look like American bobcats (*Lynx rufus*). The founding member, named Pixie, was born to an unusually tall, bobtailed male – rumoured to have been sired by a bobcat – and a domestic female. However, DNA testing has not detected any bobcat genes. Regardless, much like bobcats, Pixiebobs have a stocky, muscular body with a soft, woolly coat. Their tails can range in length – from non-existent to a full tail – but should be at least 5cm (2in) and reach the hock (or ankle) for showing. These cats are said to be good-natured and make good companions for almost any type of household, including those with children or other pets. They take happily to family life, enjoy taking part in activities, playing games and snuggling in bed.

ABOVE:
Extra toes
Pixiebobs commonly have extra toes on their paws – a condition called polydactylism – which is considered lucky and accepted in this breed standard.

SHORTHAIR

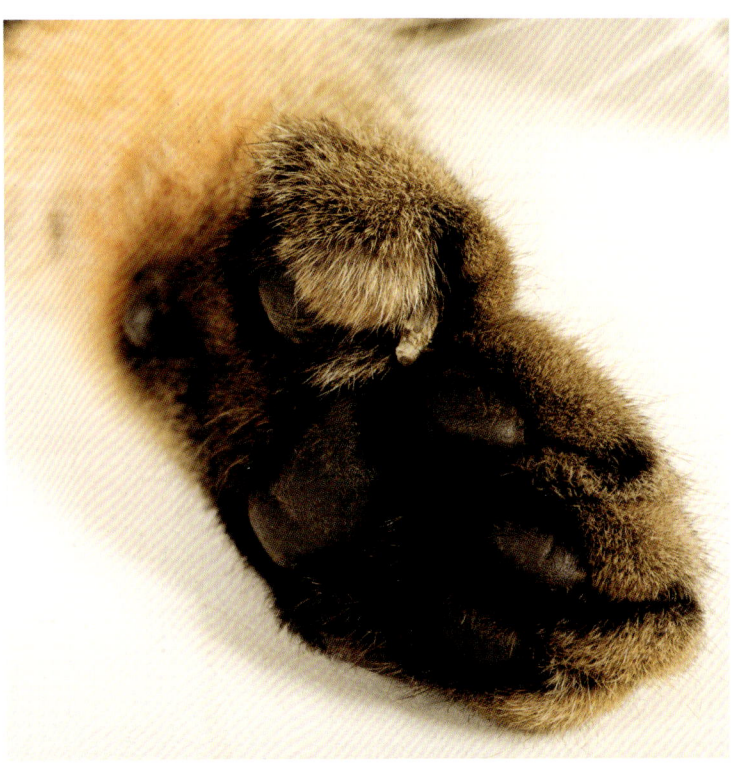

ALL PHOTOGRAPHS:
Pixiebob
Like bobcats, Pixiebobs have a bobbed tail and ear tufts, but these laid-back cats love to be part of a human family.

Russian Blue

With striking green eyes and a distinctive blue coat, the Russian Blue is believed to have originated in the port of Archangel in Russia and was brought to Northern Europe by sailors in the 1860s. Rumours also abound that the Russian Blue descended from the cats kept by the Russian czars. Exhibited as 'Archangel Cat', the Russian Blue was also among the contestants in the first cat show held in England in the 1870s. From the 1960s, the Russian Blue began gaining popularity. This gentle and loyal cat develops strong bonds with its family and loves a good routine. Though friendly, it tends to be rather reserved and can be wary of strangers or unknown guests. Quietly affectionate, the Russian Blue is content with spending some time alone in a calm environment. Besides blue, the Russian is bred in other colours and patterns: white, black and tabby. These colour varieties, also known as the Russian Shorthairs, were developed in a specific Australian breeding programme in the 1970s, but most breed organisations do not recognise them. The UK's Governing Council of the Cat Fancy (GCCF) has distinct breed standards for the Russian Blue, Russian White and Russian Black.

CHARACTERISTICS

Coat
Blue only
Weight
3.6–6.8kg (8–15lb)
Lifespan
10–20 years
Personality
Gentle, intelligent, friendly
Origin
Russia

LEFT:
Cuddly
This striking cat is noted for its green eyes and plush, bluish-grey coat that makes it look cuddly.

ABOVE:
Shades of grey
The coat of the Russian Blue varies from a light shimmering silver to a darker, slate grey or blue.

SHORTHAIR

ALL PHOTOGRAPHS:
Lucky charm
According to folklore, Russian Blue cats were kept with newborns to chase away evil spirits.

BOTH PHOTOGRAPHS:
Smiling mouth
The Russian blue has beautiful green eyes and a slightly upturned mouth, which gives it a subtle smile.

SHORTHAIR

Savannah

CHARACTERISTICS

Coat
Black or black smoke (often with ghost-spotting), brown-spotted tabby, black silver-spotted tabby
Weight
3.5–11kg (8–24lb)
Lifespan
12–20 years
Personality
Confident, outgoing, curious
Origin
United States

This stunning spotted cat, with huge ears and long legs, gets its exotic look from the serval – a native wild cat of the African plains known to be a remarkable leaper. The first Savannah cat was born in 1986, after a chance mating between a male serval (*Leptailurus serval*) and a female Siamese. The cat – fittingly named Savannah – had the perfect combination of wild and domestic traits from its parents, and was later bred with several other domestic cats to develop the breed further. Except for its wild looks, the Savannah has a somewhat wild demeanour and is best suited for experienced owners. This extremely energetic and curious cat needs plenty of space to play, explore, run and jump – in fact, it is known to jump up to about 2.5m (8ft) in the air! It can also be found opening doors or cupboards, turning on taps and even flushing the toilet. But Savannah cats are loyal and closely bond with their families too – though do not expect them to sit on laps. The International Cat Association (TICA) officially recognized the Savannah in 2012, but some countries and states impose restrictions on owning these cats due to their wild cat ancestry.

ABOVE:
African plains
A cross between the wild serval and the domestic cat, the Savannah was named after the lush plains of Africa, where the serval lives.

ABOVE:
Tallest cat
Savannah cats have the longest legs of domestic cats. In fact, a Savannah cat named Arcturus is the world's tallest cat, measuring just over 48cm (19in).

SHORTHAIR

ABOVE AND OPPOSITE:
Innate pouncer
The spotted Savannah owes most of its looks and hunting abilities to the wild serval. Like its ancestor, it can suddenly spring onto its prey.

SHORTHAIR
Scottish Fold

Named for its place of origin and unusual ears, the Scottish Fold comes in both short- and long-haired versions. Its unique ears fold forward and fit closely to the skull, giving it an almost owl-like look. The first Scottish Fold was a white, long-haired barn cat named Susie discovered on a Scottish farm in 1961. Breeders took interest and the Scottish Fold was developed by crossing Scottish Folds with other cats, such as the British Shorthairs and American Shorthairs. The folded ears – a result of a natural mutation – are passed on to about half of the kittens. The others are left with straight ears and are known as Scottish Straights. However, the gene responsible for the folded ears is associated with certain skeletal problems and, thus, some breed registries do not approve of these cats and several countries prohibit their breeding. Regardless, the rare Scottish Folds are known for being sweet, loyal and sociable, who thrive on the attention and affection of their owners.

CHARACTERISTICS
Coat
Most colours and patterns
Weight
2.7–5.9kg (6–13lb)
Lifespan
11–14 years
Personality
Sweet, affectionate, loyal, sociable
Origin
United Kingdom

ABOVE:
Lops
Scottish Folds were first known as lop-eared, or lops, after the lop-eared rabbit, until 1966.

RIGHT
All round
This rounded, medium-sized cat is compact and solid, with a round head and large round eyes.

Intriguing ears
Though the folded ears are a distinctive feature, some Scottish Folds do not develop them. These are named Scottish Straights.

ALL PHOTOGRAPHS:
Folded ears
All Scottish Fold kittens are born with straight ears that begin to fold within about three weeks.

SHORTHAIR

ABOVE:
Teddy bear
The easy-going, affectionate Selkirk Rex resembles a soft, stuffed toy that you just want to pick up and hug!

Selkirk Rex

CHARACTERISTICS

Coat
All colours and patterns
Weight
4.1–7.3kg (9–16lbs)
Lifespan
10–15 years
Personality
Affectionate, easy-going, playful
Origin
United States

With a distinctive curly coat, the Selkirk Rex originated with a curly-coated kitten, known as Miss DePesto, that was born in an American animal shelter in 1987. This curly-coated kitten, whose siblings all had straight fur, also had the curly whiskers for which the Selkirk Rex is known. The breed was developed into both short-haired and long-haired by crossing the curly cats with American Shorthairs, Exotic Shorthairs, British Shorthairs, Persians and Himalayans. Like this, the medium-to-large-sized Selkirk Rex comes in many colours and patterns. Its rounded head, large eyes and dense, plush, curly coat make it look like a teddy bear. And, fortunately, it doesn't mind the love, cuddles and attention. The Selkirk Rex is generally laid-back and placid, yet still loves to play and enjoys the company of its family – it even gets along with children and other pets too.

ABOVE:
Curly or not curly?
In a litter of Selkirk Rex kittens, some will have a curly coat and some a straight one. It can take two years for the curly kittens to get their full curls.

SHORTHAIR

Plenty of curls
Unlike some other curly-coated breeds, the cuddly Selkirk Rex has erratic curls or waves in its dense, soft coat. It typically also has more curls around its neck and belly.

SHORTHAIR

Serengeti

This exotically spotted cat – inspired to resemble the wild African serval (*Leptailurus serval*) – stands out with its large ears and long legs and neck. However, unlike the Savannah, the Serengeti has no serval in its blood. Instead, it was created by crossing a Bengal and an Oriental Shorthair in California in the mid-1990s. Today, the Serengeti is being bred in several other countries, in addition to the United States, such as the United Kingdom, Australia and Russia. Serengeti cats are registered by The International Cat Association (TICA) and can be shown as a preliminary new breed. Lithe, elegant and agile, the Serengeti has a touch of wild from the Bengal and loves to jump and climb up to high places. These cats thrive on attention, though it takes them some time to warm up to new people and animals. In fact, they are incredibly loyal and talkative once they have, and have earned the nickname *velcro cats* since they adore the company and never leave the owners' side.

CHARACTERISTICS
Coat
Solid black, black smoke, and spotted tabby in any shade of brown or silver
Weight
3.6–6.8kg (8–15lb)
Lifespan
9–15 years
Personality
Gentle, outgoing, playful
Origin
United States

ABOVE:
Wild-looking ears
These exceptionally large ears – which are the same length as the head – give the Serengeti a more wild cat-like appearance.

RIGHT:
Long legs
The Serengeti has among the longest legs of domestic cats and can jump up to 2.2m (7ft) in the air.

SHORTHAIR

OPPOSITE AND ABOVE:
Exotic look
This breed was developed to look like the serval without using any wild cats in the breeding programme.

Siamese

Modern Siamese cats are a type of Asian cat that can trace their origins back to Siam, now known as Thailand. Cats with similar characteristics are mentioned in ancient manuscripts from the region and a book of cat poems from 1350. The Siamese was first brought to Europe and the United States in the 1870s, where it became a popular breed and was often featured in cat shows. Many breeders began to favour a more slender look in the 1950s and after several generations of selective breeding, the body of the Siamese has become much longer and leaner. Its head also changed, becoming long and wedge-shaped with large and wide ears, which gives it a more angular look. Original Siamese cats, which have more rounded features, are now recognized by many breed organizations as a separate breed called the Thai or Wichien Maat. Sociable and loud, Siamese cats typically require a lot of attention and will also demand it. They are also affectionate, though often only form a bond with one person, to whom they become immensely loyal.

CHARACTERISTICS

Coat
Various point colours, including tabby and tortie
Weight
3.6–6.8 kg (8–15lb)
Lifespan
15–20 years
Personality
Sociable, intelligent, affectionate, vocal
Origin
Thailand (formerly Siam)

LEFT:
Traditional
Siamese cats have distinctive dark, or point, markings on the face, ears, paws and tail. This is an old-style Siamese, now known as Thai.

ABOVE:
Distinct gaze
Bright blue, almond-shaped eyes are one of the distinguishing features of Siamese cats.

OPPOSITE AND LEFT BOTTOM:
Modern Siamese
With a triangular-shaped head, large ears and blue almond-shaped eyes, these modern-style Siamese cats are the most sociable and loud of all cats. Siamese cats are intelligent, energetic and love lots of attention.

LEFT TOP AND MIDDLE:
Similar looks
Both of these cats are Oriental Shorthairs, which can be easily mistaken for Siamese cats.

SHORTHAIR
Singapura

CHARACTERISTICS

Coat
Sepia agouti (seal brown ticking on ivory ground colour)
Weight
1.8–3.6kg (4–8lb)
Lifespan
11–15 years
Personality
Energetic, intelligent, outgoing
Origin
Singapore

With a distinctive ticked coat and large eyes and ears, the often mischievous Singapura is among the smallest cat breeds in the world. This rare cat – which is about half the average-sized cat – takes its name from Singapore, where it supposedly originated in the 1970s. There is some controversy about its origins but it is widely accepted that the breed occurred naturally on the streets of Singapore, where two American breeders found some and brought them back to the United States to start a breeding programme. The breeders faced accusations that these cats resulted from an Abyssinian and Burmese cross, brought from the United States to Singapore. But after an investigation, the Cat Fanciers' Association (CFA) in the United States found no wrongdoing. Despite its small size, the Singapura has a big personality and is incredibly energetic and agile. It thrives on attention and interaction and is constantly on the lookout for high places to climb and explore. A bored Singapura will be unhappy and tends to be mischievous. While very active, these cats also enjoy resting near their owners and sometimes on their laps or shoulders.

ABOVE:
Mascot
Singapore made the Singapura cat a national tourism mascot in 1990.

ABOVE:
Questionable origins
A 2007 scientific study found very few genetic differences between Singapura and Burmese cats.

SHORTHAIR

Singapore roots
This breed's name is derived from the Malay word for Singapore, where it supposedly originated from.

Mating & Fighting

RIGHT & BELOW:
Mating
Cats become sexually mature between six and nine months. Females attract males, or tomcats, by producing scents and long wails known as caterwauls. During mating, the tomcat is on top and bites the scruff of the female's neck.

OPPOSITE TOP:
Loose skin
When cats are fighting, their loose skin can help them manoeuvre out of a position and defend themselves.

OPPOSITE BOTTOM:
Play fight
Cats will often roll around, chase or strike each other with their paws, with claws retracted. This so-called play fighting is silent and cats usually take turns.

245

Fighting & Aggression

ABOVE TOP:
Fighting
Cats are innately threatened by those from outside of their social group – especially males. Cats often fight to mate with a female and protect food, litter boxes or their territory. Typically, fights do not last very long and the loser runs away with only a few scratches and bite marks.

ABOVE BOTTOM:
Signs of aggression
When fighting, cats flatten their ears and hold them back to avoid damaging the inner parts, and puff up their fur on their backs or tails. They may also vocalize loudly and show their teeth to intimidate their opponent. Fights look like wrestling and often involve slapping and biting.

RIGHT:
Fear
In the presence of a dog, this scared cat arches its back and raises its fur to appear bigger. When frightened, cats hold their ears to the sides and flatten their whiskers against their cheeks. In contrast, when threatened, cats hold their ears back and flat and their whiskers are forward.

SHORTHAIR
Snowshoe

Named for its distinctive white paws, the snowshoe was first seen in kittens born to a Siamese cat in the 1960s in Philadelphia, Pennsylvania. The breeder was so intrigued by the paws, combined with the striking Siamese colourpoint pattern, that she began developing the new look using seal point Siamese and bicolour American Shorthair cats. The result was a cat that had the coat of an American Shorthair with the blue eyes, point colouration and personality of the Siamese – and the distinctive white paws that look like they have been dipped in snow. However, the new breed is rare because it is difficult to consistently produce the desired results that the breed standard requires. Like the Siamese, the confident, intelligent and sociable Snowshoe cats form strong bonds with their owners but tend to use their loud voices to demand attention. They dislike being left on their own and would rather be around people and other pets. It is said that they particularly love water, so don't be surprised if one jumps in the bath with you!

CHARACTERISTICS
Coat
Colourpoint with white paws
Weight
3.2–5.4kg (7–12lb)
Lifespan
9–15 years
Personality
Affectionate, intelligent, playful
Origin
United States

ABOVE:
Loyal companion
The Snowshoe makes a loving and devoted family pet.

RIGHT
Quick learner
Snowshoes are very clever and can open doors or quickly learn to play fetch – though they may even teach you!

SHORTHAIR

ABOVE:
Unique combination
This cute Snowshoe kitten was originally developed by crossing the Siamese and American Shorthair.

OPPOSITE:
Soft-voiced
This cat breed is quite talkative and generally uses a soft, melodic voice.

SHORTHAIR

ABOVE:
Tribal cat
This cat is known as *khadzonzo* by the local tribe, meaning 'looks like tree bark', because of the distinctive ring patterns on its sides.

Sokoke

CHARACTERISTICS

Coat
Ticked brown tabby

Weight
2.3–4.5kg (5–10lb)

Lifespan
12–15 years

Personality
Friendly, intelligent, curious

Origin
Kenya

Formerly known as the African Shorthair, this extremely rare breed with a ticked tabby pattern and long legs is native to the coastal Arabuko Sokoke Forest in Kenya. The Sokoke, or Sokoke Forest Cat, was developed into a standardized breed in the late 1970s from the feral cats called *khadzonzo*. These naturally occurring cats were discovered by a British Kenyan resident, who adopted two kittens and used them for breeding. Sokoke cats were later brought to Europe and the United States, and the standardized breed was first recognized by the International Feline Federation (FIFe) in 1994. The elegant and athletic Sokoke is a skilled climber and can reach great heights with ease. It remains fairly active in adulthood and enjoys playing games at almost any moment in the day. In fact, it thrives in environments that stimulate its natural behaviours, such as climbing and playing, and is happier in homes with plenty of space and interaction. These cats bond deeply with their owners and tend to be quite chatty, even comforting them after a bad day.

ABOVE:
Camouflaged pattern
These cats have a unique coat pattern in which the ticking in both the ground colour and pattern itself creates a see-through effect.

SHORTHAIR

ALL PHOTOGRAPHS:
Kenyan cats
The long, slender Sokoke cats have long legs and their eyes are usually amber to light-green.

SHORTHAIR
Sphynx

Known for its lack of fur, the rare Sphynx originated in Canada due to a naturally occurring mutation It was formerly known as the Canadian Hairless and though it appears to be completely hairless, the Sphynx, in fact, has a light covering of downy or peach fuzz on its wrinkled body. Hairless cats have been reported throughout history but it wasn't until 1966 – after the birth of a hairless male kitten in Ontario – that breeders grew fond of this new look and decided to develop it. The Sphynx was selectively bred with other hairless breeds, like the Devon Rex, as well as short-haired cats, and was finally created in the late 1970s. Exceptionally friendly and sociable, Sphynx cats form strong bonds with their owners, often craving company and demanding large amounts of attention. They hate being alone and can be quite vocal – almost having a conversation. These affectionate and devoted cats love a warm lap and are best kept indoors to be protected against the cold and sun's rays. Their skin can become naturally very oily so they need to be regularly bathed.

CHARACTERISTICS
Coat
Hairless; any colour and pattern
Weight
3.2–6.4 kg (7–14lb)
Lifespan
9–15 years
Personality
Affectionate, outgoing, playful, vocal
Origin
Canada

ABOVE:
Mythical creature
The Sphynx was thought to resemble the Egyptian sculpture of a mythical creature, the sphinx, and was named after it.

RIGHT:
Coloured skin
Hairless cats, like this Sphynx, can display any colour and pattern on their soft, wrinkled skin.

SHORTHAIR

ALL PHOTOGRAPHS:
Hair-raising
The most well-known hairless cat breed is the Sphynx. However, these cats may have patches of hair – especially on the face, legs and tail – or a downy coat.

ALL PHOTOGRAPHS:
Hair-raising

SHORTHAIR

Suphalak

Often confused with the sable-coloured Burmese, this ancient Thai breed has distinctive golden eyes and a reddish-brown, copper-like coat throughout its body. Even its whiskers are brown and its nose a rosy-brown. The Suphalak, along with the Korat and Thai (or Wichien Maat), appears in ancient manuscripts called *Tamra Maew*, or *The Cat Book Poems*, dating back to the Ayutthaya period (1351–1767). Believed to bring good luck and fortune, legend has it that Suphalak cats were taken by the Burmese King Hsinbyushin during the Burmese–Siamese War. This story is also told in Thailand to humorously explain why the Suphalak is so rare today!

While rare and not recognized by any major breed organization, the affectionate and playful Suphalak is said to make a loving companion. But this attention-seeking cat needs dedicated playtime, interaction and energy from owners – and it is not shy to make demands or show its discontentment if left alone or ignored. As it can quickly get lonely, the Suphalak wants to constantly be in the company of others, even cats or dogs.

CHARACTERISTICS

Coat
Reddish-brown / copper
Weight
3.6–6.8kg (8–15lb)
Lifespan
12–15 years
Personality
Friendly, intelligent, playful, affectionate
Origin
Thailand

LEFT:
Coat colour
The copper-coloured coat of the Suphalak is often compared to that of the tamarind fruit pods used in Thai cuisine.

ABOVE:
Sun-rayed eyes
The eyes of the Suphalak are bright yellow or gold, described in the *Tamra Maew* as shining and sprinkling sun rays.

Lounging around
The Suphalak is notably people-oriented and mostly enjoys being in the company of others – even when lounging.

SHORTHAIR
Thai Lilac, Thai Blue Point or Lilac Point

CHARACTERISTICS

Coat
Lilac and lilac or blue points
Weight
2.7–4.5kg (6–10lb)
Lifespan
15+ years
Personality
Intelligent, affectionate, demanding
Origin
Thailand

Not to be confused with the Thai or Wichien Maat, the Thai Lilac, Thai Blue Point or Lilac Point are essentially Korat cats from Thailand but in other coat colours and patterns than the typical blue. These cats were discovered in 1989 in the United Kingdom when a pink-shaded (or lilac) kitten called Jenanca Lilac Lillee was born in a Korat litter. Later more pinkish or white kittens appeared in other litters and, eventually, it became clear that Korat cats carried recessive genes for the lilac and blue or lilac point colours, which had stayed hidden for many generations. Like their blue-coated relatives, Thai cats have lithe, muscular bodies and large, expressive eyes. They thrive on attention, are affectionate (yet demanding) with their families, and typically fit into most households without any problems. However, only the UK's Governing Council of the Cat Fancy (GCCF) recognizes this Korat-type breed.

ABOVE:
Sharp memory
Like the Korat, this intelligent cat is said to have a great memory and can return home on its own.

ABOVE:
Siamese pattern
Early breeding records show that Korat kittens have been born occasionally with a Siamese-type pattern since 1959.

SHORTHAIR

Thai Blue Point
Instead of the typical blue coat, this Korat kitten has a colourpoint pattern like that seen in the Siamese.

SHORTHAIR
Thai

This elegant cat is the original, rounder-faced and thicker-bodied Siamese that still naturally occurs in Thailand. It is also known as the Wichien Maat, which can be translated to 'moon diamond' and represents its beauty. In the 1980s, efforts to preserve the traditional Siamese cat of the 1950s began, after several generations of selective breeding in the West had created a longer and leaner Siamese – often referred to as the modern-style Siamese. Both breeds have the same distinct point colouration, with light-coloured fur on their body and a darker face, ears, legs and tail. The Thai also has a few unofficial names such as *Old-Style*, *Traditional* and *Classic Siamese*, and is now recognized by most breed organizations. Like the Modern Siamese, the Thai is sociable and vocal and requires a lot of attention, often greeting its owners when they return home. It is a lively companion rather than a quiet and cuddly cat. However, the Thai doesn't require much grooming due to its short coat.

CHARACTERISTICS
Coat
Various point colours, including tabby and tortie
Weight
3.6–6.8 kg (8–15lb)
Lifespan
15–20 years
Personality
Intelligent, social, vocal, active
Origin
Thailand (formerly Siam)

ABOVE:
Full features
The Thai has fuller cheeks and a flat forehead compared to its relative the Modern Siamese.

RIGHT
Azure eyes
Like the Modern Siamese, Thai cats are known for their distinctive deep blue eyes.

SHORTHAIR

LEFT:
New name
The Thai is a new breed name that has been given to the original Siamese.

ABOVE:
Undivided attention
This highly intelligent kitten is very energetic, sociable and vocal and will demand your undivided attention.

ABOVE:
Famous face
This cat breed's face can be found on postage stamps in over 30 countries.

Tonkinese

CHARACTERISTICS

Coat
Most colours in various patterns
Weight
2.7–5.4kg (6–12lb)
Lifespan
12–16 years
Personality
Active, sociable, playful
Origin
United States

Originally referred to as the Chocolate Siamese, the Tonkinese is a cross between the Burmese and Siamese. This modern breed was developed in the 1960s–1970s to create a more 'moderate' breed that balanced the Siamese with the qualities of the Burmese. However, the Tonkinese is thought to be an ancient breed, mentioned in *The Cat Book of Poems*, and often confused with the Burmese and Siamese. It is also said that the 'Chocolate Siamese' was brought to the West in the 19th century. In addition, through genetic research, Wong Mau – often considered the first Burmese – was found to be a Burmese–Siamese cross (or Tonkinese) who came to the United States in the 1930s. Affectionate, sociable and loyal, the lean yet sturdy Tonkinese cats love the attention of their family and sitting on laps, though they are convinced that humans were made to love them and would rule the household if they could! They are not as talkative as the Siamese but will vocalize their feelings.

ABOVE:
Tonk
The Tonkinese breed is often affectionately called Tonk as a shortened nickname.

Famous face
This cat breed's face can be found on postage stamps in over 30 countries.

SHORTHAIR

Temperature-regulated
The point colouration in this kitten is regulated by temperature: cooler areas have dark markings while no pigment is produced in warmer ones.

SHORTHAIR
Toybob

One of the smallest breeds, the Toybob originated in Russia in the 1980s due to a natural genetic mutation. A stray cat that looked like a Siamese with a short, kinked tail was adopted off the streets of the Russian Rostov region in 1983. Two years later, a seal-pointed female cat with a curled bobtail was found and the two were bred to create the first Toybob cat named Kutciy. Over the next few decades, the short-tailed Toybob was developed into both short- and longhaired varieties in a wide range of colours and patterns. This small and cuddly cat with a short tail seemingly remains a kitten its whole life and has a big personality. Affectionate, playful and agile, it bonds closely with its owners and loves to play, while also being content to cuddle in a lap. The Toybob is officially recognized by the Cat Fanciers' Association (CFA) and registered as a preliminary new breed by The International Cat Association (TICA).

CHARACTERISTICS
Coat
Short or long; all colours and patterns
Weight
1.8–3.2kg (4–7lb)
Lifespan
14–20 years
Personality
Gentle, affectionate, playful, sociable
Origin
Russia

ABOVE:
Toy-bob
Toybobs are named for their small, or 'toy', size and bobbed tail that can be kinked, curved or slightly straight.

RIGHT:
Popular companion
A Toybob's personality and small, cuddly size make this breed popular as a companion pet.

Toyger

This wild-looking breed was developed in the 1990s to resemble a small or 'toy' tiger and raise awareness of tiger conservation. To get the tiger-marked coat, a striped short-haired cat was crossed with a Bengal. In addition to its vertical stripes, the Toyger also moves gracefully and confidently like a big cat. These rare and medium-sized cats are long, sleek and muscular but not bulky, though the females tend to be smaller and less muscular than males. Intelligent, sociable and outgoing, Toyger cats adore their families and easily bond with people of all ages, as well as other animals. They are naturally active and athletic yet also laid-back so will live happily as house cats, if they have plenty of space and interaction with their owners. Always ready to play, Toyger cats can be taught to play games like fetch, do tricks and walk on a lead.

LEFT:
Glittery coat
The coat of the Toyger has a glitter-like sheen that accentuates the bold colour and unique tiger-marked pattern.

ABOVE:
Perfect combination
This designer cat combines the striking striped coat of a tiger with the amiable temperament of a domestic cat.

CHARACTERISTICS

Coat
Brown mackerel tabby
Weight
3.6–6.8kg (8–15lb)
Lifespan
9–15 years
Personality
Intelligent, laid-back, affectionate
Origin
United States

Tricks
Keen to learn, this breed can be taught tricks and skills through careful instruction and practice from its owners.

SHORTHAIR
Ukrainian Levkoy

CHARACTERISTICS

Coat
Hairless or very fine hair; any colour and pattern

Weight
3.6–6.8kg (8–15lb)

Lifespan
12–15 years

Personality
Curious, playful, affectionate

Origin
Ukraine

A cross between the Scottish Fold and Donskoy, this unusual and rare breed was intentionally created in Ukraine in the 2000s. It has inward-folding ears from the Scottish Fold, while the hairless Donskoy gave it little to no hair. Later in its development, the Ukrainian Levkoy was also crossed with Sphynx, Oriental Shorthair and domestic cats. Although the Ukrainian Levkoy is a hairless breed, it can have some hair that should be fine and downy. An excess of its soft, elastic skin also gives it a wrinkled appearance. Sociable and playful, Ukrainian Levkoy cats require plenty of attention in return for their affection. They will never turn down a game and can be found climbing and exploring every corner of your home. Often described as dog-like, these cats are not only loyal and devoted companions but their distinctive angular faces and inward-folding ears make them look like puppies! So far, only Ukrainian and Russian cat fanciers and breed organizations recognize the Ukrainian Levkoy.

ABOVE:
Levkoy plant
This breed was named Levkoy for its folded ears, which resemble the bent leaves of the Levkoy plant.

ABOVE:
Downy fur
Like this cute kitten, many Ukrainian Levkoy cats have light, downy fur instead of being completely hairless.

Stepped profile
The Ukrainian Levkoy has a distinctive angular-shaped head with curly whiskers and a 'stepped' profile.

SHORTHAIR
Ural Rex

This rare breed originates from the Ural regions of Russia, as its name suggests. The founder was a black and white wavy-haired kitten – named Vasily – born to straight-haired cats in the late 1980s. Like in other rex cats, the wavy coat is the result of a genetic mutation. However, this seems to be different from that found in the Cornish Rex, Devon Rex or German Rex. The Ural Rex has a soft, dense double coat that can be short or long with distinctive elastic, close-lying waves. These unique waves can take up to two years to fully develop, although the first curls appear at the age of three to four months. Besides its waves, the Ural Rex is known for its friendly, calm nature and playful disposition. This quiet and affectionate cat loves to spend time with people of all ages and other pets, making it an excellent companion. After careful development, the Ural Rex was internationally recognized by the World Cat Federation in 2006.

CHARACTERISTICS
Coat
Wavy or curly; various colours and patterns
Weight
3.6–6.8kg (8–15lb)
Lifespan
12–16 years
Personality
Friendly, playful, affectionate
Origin
Russia

ABOVE:
Curly coat
Ural Rex kittens are typically born with a curly coat, but their curls disappear until they are about 3-4 months old.

RIGHT
Kitten-hood waves
The unique waves of the Ural Rex form in kitten-hood; their half-closed curls turn into even waves at 6-7 months.

Longhair

Cats are also known for their long, luxurious coats. These coats can reach up to 12cm (5in) and range from semi-long to extremely plush and flowing. It is believed that the long hair in domestic cats was caused by a natural mutation. Cats with fluffy coats first appeared in colder, isolated regions, most likely to deal with the harsh environment. During the 16th century, the first long-haired cats were imported into Europe from Asia Minor, Persia and Russia. Specifically, the ravishing Turkish Angoras are thought to be the original long-haired cats – though not as we know them today. Turkish Angoras were very popular until the 19th century when people started preferring the Persians. Though Persians remain one of the favourites, other longhairs are becoming increasingly popular. What's more, rare long-haired breeds with unusual ears or curly fur have been developed by crossing the shorthair version with longhair breeds. But while these fluffy cats are beautiful – and extra fun to cuddle, if that is what they like – they require more maintenance than shorthairs. So be prepared for frequent grooming to prevent mats and tangles, and to often find hair on couches and carpets!

OPPOSITE:
Ragamuffin
This big, fluffy cat is a wonderful companion, known for its docile nature and thick, luscious coat.

LONGHAIR
American Bobtail

Despite resembling wild cats, the American Bobtail is not a mix between a house cat and a bobcat. Its origins can be traced back to the feral domestic cats in the United States that had natural bobbed tails. The only outcrosses allowed in this breed are non-pedigree domestic cats – both long-haired and short-haired. This makes the gene pool extremely diverse and most breeders no longer use feral short-tailed cats in their breeding programmes.

The sturdy native American breed, which also comes in a short-haired version, has a distinctive shortened tail which measures about 2.5–10cm (1–4in) long. Its large, almost almond-shaped eyes, and distinct brow above them, give the American Bobtail a wild cat's hunting gaze and alert expression. But it is harmless and an excellent, devoted companion in any living environment – including in family homes with children, alongside travellers, in trucks and sailboats. American Bobtails are even used in therapy. And luckily, its long coat does not mat, which makes it easy to groom.

CHARACTERISTICS

Coat
All colours and patterns, with or without white

Weight
3.2–7.3kg (7–16lb)

Lifespan
11-15 years

Personality
Affectionate, sociable, adaptable, intelligent

Origin
United States

ABOVE:
Late maturity
Though adorable, it takes 2-3 years for an American Bobtail to reach adult size.

RIGHT
Shaggy coat
Long-haired American Bobtails have slightly shaggy fur and is usually somewhat longer around their neck, belly, legs and tail.

LONGHAIR

ABOVE:
Mutation
The American Curl is known for its unusual shaped ears, thanks to a natural mutation.

American Curl

CHARACTERISTICS

Coat
All colours and patterns
Weight
2.3–4.5kg (5–10lb)
Lifespan
10-20 years
Personality
Curious, friendly, affectionate
Origin
United States

This designer cat breed originated in Southern California, after a black long-haired, curly-eared stray – taken in by a family in 1981 – had a litter of kittens with the same unusual ears. A breeding programme was later developed for both long-haired and short-haired forms. As the name suggests, the American Curl's ears curve backwards. These smoothly turn back at least 90 degrees, as a result of a natural mutation.

All American Curls have silky coats that lie close against their bodies, but those with a long coat also have a beautiful long, plumed tail. These small-to-medium-sized cats do not shed that much and grooming is easy, thanks to their little undercoat. This breed, noted for its affectionate and friendly personality, makes an ideal family cat. However, it will want to be with you all the time and, though easy-going and not especially talkative, it will ask for attention or playtime when needed.

ABOVE:
Ear shape
American Curl kittens are born with straight ears, but these may begin to curl within a few days.

LONGHAIR

Curled ears
The ears of the American Curl should not be handled because the cartilage could break.

LONGHAIR

Balinese

Named after the graceful dancers of Bali, the Balinese is a long-haired version of the Siamese. Records, as early as the 1920s, show that long-haired kittens occasionally popped up in Siamese litters. However, these were considered a fault and quietly sold as pets. It wasn't until the 1950s, in the United States, that the Balinese – with its long, silky coat, sapphire-blue eyes and a distinctive plumed tail – was developed into a new breed.

Like the Siamese, the Balinese could have either an old-style or modern body type. And initially, the Balinese was recognized in only four point colours: seal, blue, chocolate and lilac. Then more colours – including red and cream – and tabby (or lynx) and tortie patterns were added, but some registries considered these cats as the separate Javanese breed. An affectionate, attention-seeking cat, the Balinese loves being around its family – so much so, that it becomes demanding and should never be left alone for too long. If so, the lively, intelligent and mischievous Balinese will make you regret it!

CHARACTERISTICS

Coat
Many point colours, including seal, blue, chocolate and lilac

Weight
2.3–5.4kg (5–12lb)

Lifespan
18–22 years

Personality
Outgoing, curious, affectionate, vocal, intelligent, mischievous

Origin
Thailand / United States

ABOVE:
Modern type
With its wedge-shaped head and long, large ears, this kitten has distinctly modern-type traits. The CFA would recognize this tabby-pointed kitten as a Balinese-Javanese.

RIGHT:
Old-style Balinese
Also known as traditional or "apple-head", the old-style Balinese has a rounder head and body. This type closely resembles the original cats from the early breeding programmes.

LONGHAIR

ABOVE:
Albinism
The white parts of a point pattern is in fact a type of albinism – a reduced or lack of the pigment that normally gives colour. Only the coolest parts of this cat's body has developed colour!

RIGHT:
Close-fitting coat
The silky, one-layered coat of a Balinese lies close to the body and rarely tangles or mats. This means this long-haired breed is relatively easy to groom.

LONGHAIR

Stunning sight
With a silky coat and stunning sapphire-blue eyes, this long-haired version of the Siamese is highly sociable, inquisitive and often mischievous.

Birman

This striking colourpoint breed, also known as the Sacred Cat of Burma, is noted for its sapphire-blue eyes, slightly curved 'Roman' nose and white paws. Believed to have originated in Burma, legend has it that the Birman acquired its eyes from a blue-eyed goddess as a reward for protecting a priest in ancient Burma – the country now known as Myanmar. She also gave the Birman a gold-tinted coat but left its paws white, as a symbol of purity. Though the true story of the Birman is largely unknown, it is likely that this breed was transported to France, where it was developed in the 1920s. Its name comes from the French *Birmanie* meaning Burma.

Gentle and sweet, the Birman is a loving companion that fits in well with almost any household. This lap cat adores being around people – in fact, it doesn't like to be left alone – and usually gets along with children and other pets. While Birmans have soft voices, they frequently make chirp-like meows to get attention and can converse with their owner.

LEFT:
Single coat
Despite its long, silky-textured coat, the gorgeous Birman has a single coat which means it lacks an undercoat and is quite easy to groom.

ABOVE:
Point markings
Birman kittens are born completely white, then gradually develop points of colour after 1-2 weeks. These point markings reach full colour when the cats are 2 years old.

CHARACTERISTICS

Coat
All colour points, with white paws
Weight
2.7–6.8kg (6–15lb)
Lifespan
12–16 years
Personality
Easy-going, gentle, affectionate
Origin
Possibly Myanmar (formerly Burma) / France

LONGHAIR

Birman
With distinctive sapphire-blue eyes, white paws, a Roman nose and a long silky coat, this precious colourpoint kitten enjoys human company.

Tongue

Papillae
Papillae act like a hair comb and allow large amounts of saliva to get to different layers of fur and right down to the skin for a deep clean. They also help detangle cats' fur.

Grooming

RIGHT:
Bonded
Cats groom each other only when they already have a social bond. This is known as allogrooming or social grooming, and is a sign of affection. Cats learn this behaviour from their mothers, meaning that a maternal instinct could likely play a role, too.

BELOW:
Grooming
Cats spend up to 50 per cent of their day licking their coats. This keeps them clean and smooth, which helps protect their skin from infections. Cats begin by licking their paws for cleaning their head and then work their way down the body.

OPPOSITE:
Purr-fectly clean
A cat grooms its belly inside the house to keep its fur clean. It will lick, pull and bite at its fur to remove dead skin, hair, any detritus or parasites.

LONGHAIR

British Longhair

CHARACTERISTICS

Coat
Many colours and patterns

Weight
3.2–7.7kg (7–17lb)

Lifespan
14–20 years

Personality
Affectionate, easy-going, calm

Origin
United Kingdom

As the name suggests, this long-haired cat originated in the United Kingdom. Except for its longer coat, it shares the same features as its cousin, the British Shorthair. In the mid-20th century, British Shorthairs were crossed with Persians, among others, to refine and standardize the breed. This resulted in unwanted long-haired kittens in the litter, which are now intentionally bred as the British Longhair. However, only a few registries consider the British Longhair to be a separate breed and the naming is quite inconsistent. For example, the Feline Federation Europe (FFE) confusingly calls it the Highlander – another short-haired and long-haired breed.

Known to be quite loving, easy-going and calm, British Longhairs can live happily in almost any household and do not mind some alone time. Whilst not overly talkative or demanding, these cats will want to get involved in the family routines and ensure these are done properly and on time. They generally like their space in calm environments, though also enjoy the attention. When relaxing, these quietly affectionate cats can usually be found sitting close to their owners rather than on their laps, but like a cuddle on their own terms.

ABOVE:
Teddy bear
British Longhairs have a distinctive round head, round cheeks and large round eyes that makes them look like cuddly teddy bears!

ABOVE:
Plush
The large and stocky British Longhair sports a plush, semi-long coat, and a similar face to its Shorthair cousin.

LONGHAIR

Different names
The British Longhair is also known as the Britannica in some parts of Europe and the Lowlander in the United States.

LONGHAIR

Chantilly-Tiffany

This attractive breed is often thought of as a long-haired Burmese, but these are not related at all – despite the once widespread false belief that the Burmese was included in its ancestry. The Chantilly-Tiffany started in New York, in the late 1960s, with the litters of two chocolate-brown long-haired cats of unknown origin. And around the same time, in the early 1970s, a similar litter was born in Canada. It acquired many names during its development – Foreign Longhair, Tiffany and Chantilly – which caused considerable confusion. Despite the many efforts, this unlucky, gentle breed remained rare throughout its life and never really got off the ground. It was considered an easy-going, loyal and affectionate companion that was not overly demanding or mischievous. Usually forming a strong bond with one particular person in the family, it asked for attention with soft chirps or trills. However, since 2015, the Chantilly-Tiffany is considered extinct with no breeders, no breeding programmes and no records of any surviving or un-neutered cats left.

CHARACTERISTICS
Coat
Black, chocolate, cinnamon, fawn, blue and lilac; various tabby patterns
Weight
2.7–5kg (6–11lb)
Lifespan
7–16 years
Personality
Gentle, affectionate, quiet
Origin
North America

ABOVE:
Devoted
This soft-voiced cat was a devoted family member, who got on well with children and other pets. It loved the attention, constantly followed its owner around, and could be quite chatty.

RIGHT
Soft and silky
Chantilly-Tiffany cats had a soft and silky coat that took about two years to reach full length. The first cats were a deep chocolate with golden eyes, but other coat colours were later accepted.

Sweet face
This gentle cat has a broad, modified wedge-shaped head with high cheekbones.

LONGHAIR

ABOVE:
Same litter
Both long-haired and short-haired kittens may appear in the same litter of either Cymric or Manx cats.

Cymric

CHARACTERISTICS

Coat
All colours and patterns

Weight
3.6–5.4kg (8–12lbs)

Lifespan
14-16 years

Personality
Gentle, playful, sociable, intelligent

Origin
United Kingdom / Canada

Also called the Longhair Manx, this affectionate and clever breed is a long-haired version of the tailless Manx. Some cat breed registries consider the Cymric a long-haired variety of the Manx, others a separate breed. Besides their coat length, the Cymric and Manx are essentially the same cat – both have rounded bodies and naturally occurring short or no tails at all. However, even though the Manx is native to the Isle of Man and long-haired kittens have appeared in its litters for centuries, the Cymric was intentionally developed as a new breed in Canada, in the 1960s.

Cymrics enjoy the company of people, including children, and other pets. Sociable and playful – but not overly energetic or demanding – they can learn to perform tricks and will amuse themselves while the family is at work or school. Cymrics are also powerful jumpers due to their long back legs and muscular build. Though these cats are known for their lack of tail, some have short tails and a few might even have long tails. In fact, a fully tailed Cymric is only recognized as a separate breed – called Isle of Man Longhair – by the New Zealand Cat Fancy (NZCF).

ABOVE:
What's in the name
The Welsh word for Wales is Cymru, which lends itself to this breed's name. Though the breed is not associated with Wales, the breeders wanted a Celtic-sounding name.

LONGHAIR

LONGHAIR

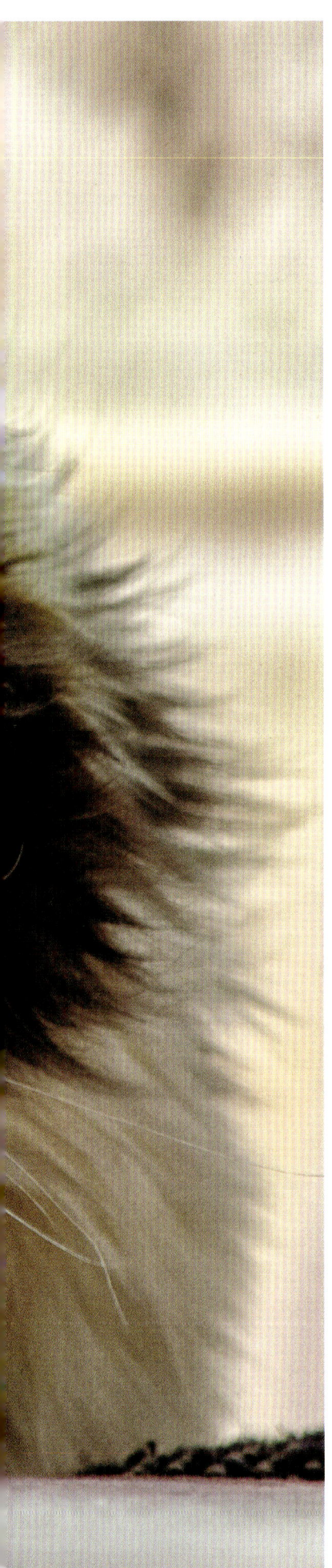

LEFT:
Cymric
Though the Manx is native to the Isle of Man, the Cymric was developed later in Canada.

ABOVE TOP AND BOTTOM:
Tail types
Similar to the Manx, Cymrics have distinct tail types according to their length: the entirely tailless 'rumpy'; a short knob of a tail or 'rumpy-riser'; a 'stumpy' , which is a curved or kinked tail; and the type with the nearly normal-length tail, the 'longy'.

LONGHAIR

Highlander

With its dense, shaggy coat and bobbed or short tail, the Highlander looks like a small bobcat. However, no wild cats were used to develop the breed in 2004 and there is nothing wild about its personality. This affectionate, friendly and people-oriented cat loves to play and hang out with the family. In fact, it will never turn down a chance to play and will happily get along with children, other cats or cat-friendly dogs – as long as it is at the centre of attention. Except for playing, these exceptionally active cats love to explore and climb. Highlander cats do not like to be left alone for long periods and will also most likely follow you quietly around the house all day. There are both long-haired and short-haired versions, though the longhair's coat needs more attention – especially with the longer shaggy belly hair – to keep it free from tangles and matting.

CHARACTERISTICS

Coat
All colours in tabby pattern, including colourpoints

Weight
4.5–9.1kg (10–20lb)

Lifespan
10–15 years

Personality
Affectionate, gentle, playful, energetic

Origin
United States

ABOVE:
Ball of fur
This adorable ball of fur with loosely curled ears was originally called the Highlander Lynx.

RIGHT:
Wild-looking
Despite resembling a wild bobcat with its long tabby coat, the Highlander is entirely domestic.

LONGHAIR

Straight ears
Highlander cats are known for their curled ears and short tails, but some can be born with straight ears and a long tail.

LONGHAIR

LONGHAIR

Play sessions
Highlander cats are very playful and can be taught numerous tricks – even how to play fetch!

Himalayan

Also known as the Colourpoint Persian, this beautiful cat is the result of crossing long-haired Persians with the Siamese. Long-drawn-out attempts to produce Persians with Siamese markings go back to the 1930s, but the Himalayan was recognized as a breed in the 1950s. As the breed developed, the Himalayan kept looking less like the Persian so efforts to re-establish the breed along the Persian lines began in the 1970s. However, this led to the breed being recognized as a colour variant of the Persian in many breed organizations, rather than a separate breed.

Like the Persian, the Himalayan is a calm cat that is sweet and quiet. It may get a burst of energy at times, but otherwise, the Himalayan can be found sleeping in the sun or sitting in a lap – it loves to be cuddled or petted and enjoys attention from its family. They are happy in any home, as long as it is fairly quiet, playtime is scheduled and owners are generally gentle. However, the Himalayan's fluffy coat is not easy and requires daily grooming to prevent tangles and mats.

CHARACTERISTICS

Coat
White to cream with colour, tabby or tortie patterned points
Weight
2.7–6.8kg (6–15lb)
Lifespan
12–15 years
Personality
Sweet, gentle, calm, affectionate
Origin
United States

LEFT:
Mixed-breed
The Himalayan gets its long, silky fur from the Persian, while its colourpoint coat and blue eyes are thanks to the Siamese.

ABOVE:
Earned name
Himalayans are not named after the mountain range in Asia. In fact, this striking long-haired breed earned its name from the Himalayan rabbit due to the coat's similar appearance.

LONGHAIR

ABOVE:
Persian-like
Similar to the Persian, the Himalayan has a round head with a short, snub nose and large blue eyes, a short, stubby body and legs, and a long thick coat.

RIGHT:
Playtime
Himalayans are playful cats too and need daily playtime, so don't let their laid-back, calm personalities fool you. They will get into mischief if they become bored!

Fluffy kitten
This litter of precious newborn kittens look like little fluffy balls of fur.

LONGHAIR

Striking stare
The Himalayan has a round, cobby body with long, lush fur and short legs, and brilliant blue eyes.

LONGHAIR

LONGHAIR
Balinese-Javanese

CHARACTERISTICS

Coat
Many point colours, and in tabby and tortie patterns
Weight
2.3–5.4kg (5–12lb)
Lifespan
18–22 years
Personality
Outgoing, curious, affectionate, vocal, intelligent, mischievous
Origin
Thailand / United States

This charming cat was developed in the late 1970s to introduce more colours and patterns in the Balinese – essentially a long-haired Siamese that was originally recognized only in seal, blue, chocolate and lilac. However, the American Cat Fanciers' Association (CFA) had already classified the short-haired Siamese cats in other colour points, such as red and cream, and tortie and tabby (also known as lynx) point patterns, as a separate breed called the Colourpoint Shorthair. So this long-haired cat, derived mostly from the Colourpoint Shorthair, was also considered a separate breed – the Javanese. But while other registries included new pointed colours and patterns in the Balinese, it wasn't until 2008 that the CFA made the Javanese a colour division of the Balinese.

Active, curious and extremely loving, the Javanese is like its parent breeds – the Siamese, Balinese and Colourpoint Shorthair. When it is not prying into every hole and corner of the house, it enjoys following its owner around. Though not as loud as the Siamese, this talkative cat demands attention, tricks and games. With its high energy levels, the Javanese needs plenty of activity, company and amusement to remain happy.

ABOVE:
Java Island
The Javanese was named after the Indonesian island of Java, which is next to Bali.

ABOVE:
Graceful appearance
This svelte cat has a long, graceful body with slim-boned legs, yet is strong and muscular.

LONGHAIR

Point colouration
Like all colourpoint cats, the Balinese-Javanese is born white and then develops darker points in the colder parts of its body, including the face, ears, paws and tail.

LONGHAIR
Kinkalow

This designer dwarf breed, which also comes in a short-haired version, was created in the 1990s by crossing the short-legged Munchkin with the curly-eared American Curl. The Kinkalow is thought to be named for its *kinked* ears and *low*-to-the-ground stature. Except for these two distinctive traits, the Kinkalow's tail is sometimes longer than the length of its body, too. Kinkalow cats are still experimental and only recognized by the smaller breed organization, the Rare and Exotic Feline Registry (REFR). Regardless of its official status, this rare, miniature cat is said to make an excellent pet for every type of family with its playful and people-loving temperament. It enjoys sticking close to its owners, playing with them and resting on their laps. The Kinkalow also always wants to know everything that is happening around them – it will even follow you into the bathroom! Its semi-long, shaggy coat needs regular grooming to keep it tangle-free.

CHARACTERISTICS
Coat
Many colours and patterns
Weight
2.7–4.1kg (6–9lb)
Lifespan
12–15 years
Personality
Affectionate, playful, intelligent
Origin
United States

ABOVE:
Traits
This Kinkalow kitten has the distinctive curled-back ears and short legs. But not all kittens do; some are born with normal-length legs and straight ears.

RIGHT
Small
Many Kinkalow cats stay small their entire lives and never grow to be more than 20cm (8in) tall from paw to shoulder.

LONGHAIR

Curious
This adorable Kinkalow kitten sits on a stone. Cats are curious by nature and being outside gives them a chance to explore and to be kept mentally stimulated.

LONGHAIR

ABOVE:
Hunter
This rare, stocky breed with an unusual tail is known as an excellent hunter and fish catcher.

Kurilian Bobtail

CHARACTERISTICS

Coat
Most solid colours; bicolour, tortie and tabby patterns

Weight
3.6–6.8kg (8–15lb)

Lifespan
15–20 years

Personality
Gentle, sociable, intelligent

Origin
Kuril Islands, Sakhalin Island, Kamchatka peninsula

Native to the Kuril Islands, Sakhalin Island and the Kamchatka peninsula, this short-tailed breed was brought to mainland Russia in the mid-20th century by military personnel and scientists, where it became very popular. While also popular in some parts of Europe, it is still largely unknown in North America. Every Kurilian Bobtail has a unique, naturally occurring tail that varies in shape and length, but is never longer than 12.7cm (5in). Intelligent and sociable, the Kurilian Bobtail typically gets along well with people and other pets, despite its often wild look. It loves to sit on laps and learn new tricks, games or tasks – it can even be trained to follow house rules, though it may or may not choose to! The Kurilian Bobtail also comes in a short-haired version but the longhair has a full, plumed tail. Both, however, have soft, silky coats that lie flat on the body and generally do not mat, so are easily maintained.

ABOVE:
Kitten litters
The average litter size is 4–6 kittens, but Kurilian Bobtails typically have 2–3 kittens in a litter.

ABOVE:
Facial features
Kurilian Bobtails have a large, round head with walnut-shaped eyes, a broad and straight nose, and prominent whisker pads.

RIGHT:
Bushy tail
The short, bushy tail of the Kurilian Bobtail consists of 2–10 vertebrae that can be shaped like a *whisk*, *spiral*, or *snag*.

LONGHAIR

LaPerm

Named for the coat, LaPerm cats often look like they have had a shaggy perm. Their coats can have tight ringlets or long corkscrew curls and come in many different colours and patterns. The LaPerm first appeared on an American farm in an otherwise normal tabby litter in the 1980s, as a result of a natural genetic mutation. It was later developed into both short-haired and long-haired versions. However, the short-haired cats usually have more waves, while long-haired LaPerms can boast tighter ringlets and curls – especially around the neck, ears and plumed-like tail.

This outgoing, active and affectionate cat makes a wonderful companion to anyone who loves interaction and cuddles, and is not gone for too long. LaPerm cats need company most of the time and to play lots of interactive games. And after a fun game with their owners, LaPerm cats curl up in the closest lap and enjoy being stroked. Although their coat is long, it does not shed or mat much and requires a quick comb a few times a week.

CHARACTERISTICS

Coat
All colours and patterns
Weight
2.7–5.4kg (6–12lb)
Lifespan
12–15 years
Personality
Active, affectionate, intelligent
Origin
United States

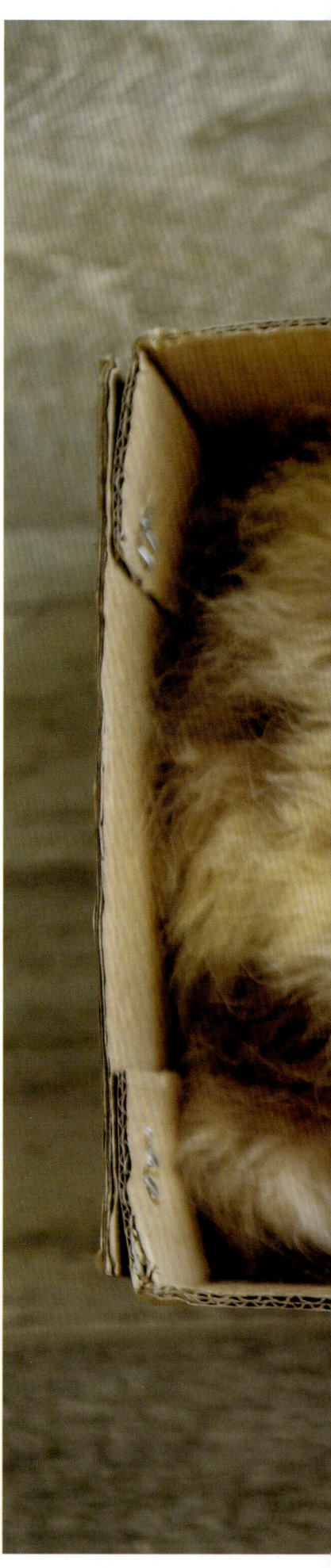

ABOVE:
Long whiskers
La Perm cats usually have the curliest fur around their necks, ears, and tails. Even their whiskers are very long and curly, unlike other rex-coated breeds that have short and brittle whiskers.

RIGHT:
Curly coat
While known for their curls, the first LaPerm cat was born completely bald. In fact, occasionally kittens are born hairless but will always grow their soft, curly coat.

Maine Coon

Native to North America, the magnificent Maine Coon is named after the US state of Maine, where it was first recognized in the 1800s. There are many theories on how exactly these cats got there – some thought they were a hybrid between feral cats and raccoons or bobcats, while others believed they were related to the Norwegian or Siberian Forest Cats. However, research has found that Maine Coons are the descendants of cats brought by Puritan settlers in the 1600–1700s. And, in fact, are closer related to cats found in the United Kingdom.

The Maine Coon, nicknamed *gentle giant*, is one of the largest cats. Its distinctive thick and waterproof coat, bushy tail and tufted ears and paws allow this cat to get through harsh winters. Since the mid-20th century, this breed has become a popular pet. Except for its incredible looks, it makes a wonderful companion due to its friendly and sweet nature. Maine Coons get along with children and other pets, including dogs, but are not big on cuddling or sitting in laps. They are also quite talkative and like to play throughout their lives – even in water.

CHARACTERISTICS

Coat
Many colours and patterns, except colourpoint
Weight
3.2–8.2kg (7–18lb)
Lifespan
9–15 years
Personality
Gentle, playful, friendly, intelligent
Origin
United States

LEFT:
Slow-maturing
The Maine Coon is slow to mature and does not reach its full potential size until it is 3–5 years old.

ABOVE:
Ear tufts
Maine Coons have longer hairs on the tips of their large ears, known as ear tufts. Quite what these hairs are for is unknown, but could be for better hearing or detecting objects.

LONGHAIR

ALL PHOTOGRAPHS:
Winter ready
The distinctive thick and waterproof coat of the Maine Coon, along with its bushy tail and tufted ears, allow this breed to get through extreme cold weather.

LONGHAIR

OPPOSITE:
Majestic Maine
This is one of the most grandiose cats with a long coat, nicknamed 'the gentle giant'.

ABOVE:
Maine kitten
This charming, fuzzy kitten with a bushy tail was the second most popular cat breed in 2023, according to the Cat Fanciers' Association (CFA).

LONGHAIR
Minuet

CHARACTERISTICS

Coat
All colours and patterns
Weight
3.2–3.6kg (7–8lb)
Lifespan
12–15 years
Personality
Easy-going, gentle, playful, curious
Origin
United States

Formerly known as the Napoleon, this round, short-legged cat was developed in the 1990s by crossing the Munchkin with Persians, Himalayans and Exotic Shorthairs. As a result, the Minuet has the very short legs of the Munchkin and the rounded face and luxuriant fur of the Persian. When the breed was first being developed, it was named the Napoleon after the French general Napoleon Bonaparte, for his supposedly small stature and fiery personality. However, in 2015, one of the major cat registries, The International Cat Association (TICA), voted to change the name to Minuet, before it fully recognized the breed.

The Minuet is said to have the gentleness of a Persian and the energy and curiosity of the Munchkin. This makes it well-suited for families, including those with children and other pets, with which it forms strong bonds and enjoys to play and cuddle. A rare breed, the Minuet comes in short-haired and long-haired versions. Both have a dense coat that can do with daily grooming – another activity that the Minuet looks forward to!

ABOVE:
Fast moving
Despite their distinctively short legs and laid-back nature, Minuets are fast-moving cats that like to dash around the house.

ABOVE:
Doll face
The Minuet gets its doll-face look from the traditional, or doll-faced, Persian, known for its sweet expression and longer nose than the peke-faced Persian.

LONGHAIR

Friendly cat
Minuets are both gentle and active cats that like to spend time with their owners.

Whiskers

Whiskers
A cat's most prominent whiskers, or vibrissae, are on each side of the nose. These are loaded with nerves at their base and are highly sensitive. Whiskers help cats navigate in the dark or 'see' up close by allowing them to locate objects through touch and air movements or vibrations. The deeply embedded whiskers are more than twice as thick as normal cat hairs.

Senses

LEFT:
Touch
Cats have long whiskers on either side of the nose, and smaller whiskers on the cheeks, above the eyes and on the back of their front legs. Through touch and air currents, cats are able to get a sense of their surroundings that helps them navigate, whereby they can detect objects or obstacles, judge the width of gaps and even measure distances between objects.

ABOVE TOP:
Hunting
A young Maine coon, renowned for its hunting skills, shows off its whiskers. When hunting, whiskers help cats detect the exact location, shape and size of their prey – especially when it is too close to their mouth and they cannot see.

ABOVE BOTTOM:
Super senses
With large eyes and ears and many whiskers, cats are adapted to be exceptional hunters – especially at dawn and dusk. Not only can they detect movement in low light, but they also have a powerful sense of smell and hearing, and their long whiskers help them navigate.

LONGHAIR
Munchkin

Known as the 'Dachshunds of the cat world', Munchkins are noted for their short legs and low-lying bodies, thanks to a natural mutation. This breed's development began in the United States in the 1980s, though records show that short-legged cats have appeared in a number of countries since the 1940s. Its name is derived from the fictional tiny residents of Munchkin Country in the 1900s book *The Wonderful Wizard of Oz*.

Despite the short legs, Munchkins can run fast, climb and often sit up on their back legs. Their shorter legs also do not appear to present any spinal problems sometimes found in short-legged dogs, like the Dachshunds. These lively and curious cats – both long-haired and short-haired – love to play, explore and socialize with people of all ages and other animals. Munchkins are only bred with other domestic cats without short legs. This means Munchkins can have varying leg lengths: the lowest-to-the-ground *rug hugger* legs, *super-short* legs that are 5–8cm (2–3in) shorter than normal, and the normal length *standard* legs.

CHARACTERISTICS

Coat
All colours and patterns
Weight
2.3–4.1kg (5–9lb)
Lifespan
15–18 years
Personality
Affectionate, curious, playful, intelligent
Origin
United States

ABOVE:
Jumping ability
The short legs of the Munchkin means it may find it hard to jump or cannot jump as high as other breeds with typically longer legs.

RIGHT
Forever short
At first glance, Munchkins may look like your average house cat. But while their bodies do grow, their legs remain short during their lifetime.

Spirited cat
This sociable short-legged cat is lively and loves playing with toys.

LONGHAIR

ABOVE:
Eye colour
A Nebelung's wide-set, striking eyes can range from yellowish-green to green as an adult.

Nebelung

CHARACTERISTICS

Coat
Blue – sometimes with silver tips

Weight
3.5–6.5kg (7.7–14.3lb)

Lifespan
11-16+ years

Personality
Affectionate, gentle, somewhat shy, playful

Origin
United States

This beautiful rare breed, with green eyes and a medium-long, dense blue coat, was developed in Denver, Colorado. In the 1980s, a black domestic shorthair cat gave birth to two separate litters, from which two stunning longhaired blue cats emerged: Siegfried and Brunhilde. These laid the foundation of the Nebelung – the name, derived from the German word Nebel meaning mist or fog, refers to its shimmering coat. Over the next decade, their descendants were bred with Russian Blues, re-creating the once-popular long-haired blue cats that were imported to England in the 19th century.

Today's Nebelung cats thrive in stable, loving and calm households – ideally with older children or senior adults, and docile pets. Lots of noise and changes can often make them anxious. Affectionate and devoted, these cats are shy with strangers and prefer the company of their own family. In fact, they tend to bond to one or two family members, often following them around. Nebelungs are happy with routine and can spend some time on their own during the day. They adore sitting on laps and often show their bellies to receive affection from owners.

ABOVE:
Mist-like creature
The blue coat can sometimes have silver-tipped hair across the whole body – in addition to only the head and shoulders. These hairs create a silvery sheen which gives the Nebelung a mist-like look.

LONGHAIR

Time for play
Nebelung cats are known for being gentle and easy-going, but also have a playful side. They particularly enjoy retrieving, jumping and climbing to high places on a regular basis.

LONGHAIR

Nebelung
Sometimes referred to as the Longhaired Russian Blue, this rare long-bodied breed with a soft, silver-tipped blue coat was developed in Colorado.

LONGHAIR
Neva Masquerade

This imposing thick-coated, rare breed is the colourpoint version of the Siberian. It is named after the Neva River in St Petersburg in Russia, where it was developed in the 1970s. With its distinctive blue eyes and dark point markings, it is believed to have come from a cross between the Siberian and Asian colourpoint breeds, such as the Siamese. However, some registries do not consider the Neva Masquerade to be a separate breed from the Siberian.

The Neva Masquerade is strong and powerfully built, yet is noted for its friendly and playful temperament. It enjoys being a part of the family and, in particular, becomes attached to children. While it will sit in your lap, it is also very active and needs space to jump and play. It can take about five years for Neva Masquerade cats to reach full maturity. This means their dense coat – which has three layers to keep them warm in extremely cold weather – also takes some time to grow. And when it does, the fur needs a fair amount of regular grooming.

CHARACTERISTICS

Coat
Very thick, triple coat in various colourpoints, including seal, blue, red, cream, tortie, tabby, silver or smoke and golden

Weight
4.5–9.1kg (10–20lb)

Lifespan
11–18 years

Personality
Friendly, playful, vocal, gentle, intelligent

Origin
Russia

ABOVE:
Colourpoint gene
On its large round face, the Neva Masquerade has blue eyes and darker ears and muzzle – all thanks to the same colourpoint gene found in Siamese cats.

RIGHT:
Winter coat
These cats have a distinctly longer coat in the winter, which they shed in spring.

Summer shedding
Neva masquerade cats will usually also shed at the end of the summer to prepare for their very dense winter coat.

Norwegian Forest Cat

Larger than the average cat, this beautiful breed with its long, dense coat is well adapted to surviving the harsh Scandinavian climate. Its ancestors are believed to date back to the time of Vikings, used in villages and on ships as a form of pest control. In Norway, where it has become the national cat, folktales and legends as early as the 16th century refer to huge long-haired cats that resemble Norwegian Forest Cats. They have even been associated with the two cats pulling Norse goddess Freya's chariot. But by the 20th century, they were nearly lost until an official breeding programme was put into place in the 1970s.

The Norwegian Forest Cat – known as skogkatt in Norwegian – makes a perfect companion for families who do not need physical contact with their cats all the time. While they want to be close to their owners, these cats do not want constant attention or petting. However, they do like to play games and, as terrific climbers, are often found in high places. It takes up to five years for Norwegian Forest Cats to reach full maturity and although they love the outdoors, they are also happy to live quietly in a home.

LEFT:
Mythical creatures
Norwegian Forest Cats are thought to be the mythical creatures, or mountain-dwelling fairy cats, which had extraordinary abilities in Norse legends.

ABOVE:
Thick coat
Norwegian Forest Cats have a thick double coat to protect them against harsh cold climates: a long, water-resistant top coat and a dense woolly undercoat for insulation.

CHARACTERISTICS

Coat
All colours and patterns, except chocolate, lilac, cinnamon, fawn and colourpoints

Weight
3.6–8.2kg (8–18lb)

Lifespan
14–16 years

Personality
Friendly, gentle, intelligent

Origin
Norway

LONGHAIR

BOTH PHOTOGRAPHS:
Snowy cat
The large and muscular Norwegian Forest Cat is a terrific climber and hunter. It is the national cat of Norway.

LONGHAIR

Oriental Longhair

CHARACTERISTICS

Coat
Many colours; tabby, tortie and bicolour patterns
Weight
3.6–6.4kg (8–14lb)
Lifespan
12–15 years
Personality
Affectionate, curious, playful, sociable, vocal
Origin
United Kingdom

Though not as popular as its short-haired cousin, the Oriental Longhair was developed in the United Kingdom in the 1960s. The breed was formerly known as the British Angora but was renamed in 2002 to avoid confusion with the Turkish Angora. However, confusingly, some breed organizations refer to the Oriental Longhair as Foreign Longhair, Javanese or Mandarin. And while for some it is a separate breed, others consider both the longhairs and shorthairs as the Oriental. The Oriental Longhair has a semi-long coat – which drapes over its elegant, slender body – and a long, plumed tail. Curious and playful, this lively breed loves playing games, leaping, climbing and exploring – especially high places to keep an eye on owners! It has also been known to open cupboards, doors and even refrigerators. Oriental Longhairs form strong bonds with their family and hate being left alone for long. Instead, they prefer an interactive home with lots of attention and affection and will let you know if they are not happy. Regular grooming is required, although their silky coat rarely tangles or mats so it is relatively easy.

ABOVE:
Ornamentals
Oriental cats, nicknamed Ornamentals, have a wide variety of colours and patterns – in fact, more than any other breed.

ABOVE:
Playful pet
Oriental Longhairs love to play and can even amuse themselves with an empty cardboard box – like this cat who is sitting in one!

LONGHAIR

OPPOSITE AND ABOVE:
People-orientated
Formerly known as the British Angora, this breed loves interacting with people and cannot be left alone for long periods.

LONGHAIR
Persian

With a distinctive round head, short muzzle and long, luxuriant coat, this glamorous breed has been very popular since the 19th century. Its exact origin is unknown, though it is believed that its ancestors came from Persia – now modern-day Iran. The first Persian cats – only in coats with one colour throughout – appeared in the very first cat show held in London in 1871. Selective breeding produced Persians in almost any coat colour and pattern, but also led to the peke-faced, or modern type, Persians with extreme flattened faces. These cats have been found to have several health problems, including breathing difficulties, because of the shape of their heads. Thus, there are efforts to preserve the older type, or traditional Persian, which has a more pronounced muzzle and is more popular with the general public.

Persians are happiest at home, either snuggled up to their owners, or occasionally alone. These calm cats enjoy playing but would rather be stroked and admired than engage in strenuous activities. This makes them fairly easy to care for, but they have one of the most difficult coats to maintain. Daily – often rather time-consuming – grooming is required to catch tangles and prevent impenetrable mats.

CHARACTERISTICS
Coat
Solid (blue, black, white, red, cream, chocolate or lilac), Chinchilla, Silver, Golden, Shaded, Smoke, Pewter, Cameo, Tortie, Tabby, Calico, Bi-colour, Himalayan (colourpoint)
Weight
2.7–6.8kg (6–15lb)
Lifespan
12–15 years
Personality
Sweet, gentle, calm, affectionate
Origin
Possibly Persia (Iran) / UK

ABOVE:
Traditional type
The doll-face, or traditional, Persian is a variety of the Persian without the extreme face features that were later developed in this breed.

RIGHT
Modern type
Persians with extremely flat faces, known as peke-faced, were developed after a natural mutation occurred in red tabby Persians in the 1950s.

ABOVE:
Golden Persian
With blue-green eyes and a coat ranging from rich apricot to golden, the Golden Persian is recognised as a new breed by some cat registries.

ABOVE TOP:
Golden coat
Some kittens are born with their ravishing golden fur, but it can take 2–3 years for Golden Persians to develop their coat colour.

ABOVE BOTTOM:
Persian Chinchilla
This silver-coated Persian takes its name from the chinchilla, a small South American rodent known for its soft white fur with black-tipped hair.

LONGHAIR

BOTH PHOTOGRAPHS:
Deceiving looks
Persian cats are gentle, loving companions even if their face makes them look a little grumpy.

Ragamuffin

Once a variant of the better-known Ragdoll, this cuddly cat became a separate breed in 1994. After the Ragdoll was first developed in the 1960s, a group of breeders wanted to add more colours, patterns and genetic variation to the breed. But the breeding was strictly controlled by the Ragdoll's founder, so these breeders set out to create their own distinctive breed and crossed Ragdolls with Persians, Himalayans and domestic long-haired cats.

The new development, the Ragamuffin – a name chosen in part as an homage to Ragdolls – is an enormous, docile lap cat that loves attention. While it wants to please owners, it also likes to be kept entertained with games or cuddles. And lucky for the Ragamuffin, its large expressive eyes and affectionate purring immediately draw you back in. Ragamuffins thrive in any loving home and make excellent companions for individuals or a family with younger children or other pets. Their dense, plush coat is extremely soft and is easily maintained from tangles.

LEFT:
RagaMuffin
Some registries spell the breed's name RagaMuffin. The 'M' is capitalised because, according to one of the founding breeders, they are big huggable, lovable Muffins!

ABOVE:
Sweet expression
Ragamuffins have a sweet expression with their large, walnut-shaped eyes. Their fur is silky soft with a ruff around the neck, plumed tail, and tufts in the ears and between the toes.

CHARACTERISTICS

Coat
All colours and patterns, except point colours

Weight
4.5–9.1kg (10–20lb)

Lifespan
12–16 years

Personality
Sweet, docile, calm

Origin
United States

LONGHAIR

Bonding time
Ragamuffins are very playful and love attention from their owners. They can become bored so are easily persuaded to play with toys or cuddle.

LONGHAIR

LONGHAIR
Ragdoll

CHARACTERISTICS

Coat
Many colours in solid, tabby and tortie points; bi-colour, mitted or colourpoint patterns

Weight
4.5–9.1kg (10–20lb)

Lifespan
12–16 years

Personality
Sweet, docile, easy-going, affectionate

Origin
United States

This beautiful, easy-to-handle lap cat was supposedly developed from a litter of kittens, born in California in the 1960s, that became limp and relaxed when picked up – like a ragdoll. With big bright blue eyes, a soft, silky coat and a long bushy tail, the Ragdoll is one of the largest breeds. However, this gentle giant has an easy, laid-back personality and loves to interact with people and other animals. It will happily play gentle games with children but also adores belly rubs and to spend time snuggled up to owners. When not in laps, these cuddly cats often follow owners around the house or closely watch their every move while relaxing.

Well-behaved and placid, they are also known to patiently wait for owners to come home – even carrying around their favourite toy in their mouths! In fact, Ragdolls can be trained to retrieve toys and enjoy doing so. This cat's fluffy double coat is not prone to matting, which makes it easy to keep up with its moderate grooming sessions.

ABOVE:
Purrfect
These sweet, affectionate and cuddly cats are perfect to share a home with — and they don't mind sharing space with children or other cats either!

LONGHAIR

ABOVE:
Floppy
When the docile Ragdolls were considered excessively 'floppy' when picked up, it was also mistakenly believed that these 'floppy' cats couldn't feel pain.

LONGHAIR

Big size
The huge, breathtaking Ragdoll does not reach its full size until about four years of age. The males are considerably bigger than the females.

LONGHAIR

BOTH PHOTOGRAPHS:
Large breed
These beautiful, easy-to-handle lap cats are one of the largest breeds.

LONGHAIR
Scottish Fold

As the name suggests, the Scottish Fold originated in Scotland and has folded ears due to a genetic mutation. Not only does this breed have an adorable round face and cute folded ears, but it also has a gentle, affectionate and friendly temperament. Like its short-haired relative, the Scottish Fold will happily live alongside children and other pets and does not need so much active engagement or strenuous exercise as other cats. Aside from its ears, the Scottish Fold is also known to sit in unusual positions: like a prairie dog to get a better view or like humans in the so-called *Buddha Sit*. However, unfortunately, this is often due to joint and cartilage problems that come with these small, folded ears. Debate swirls around the ethics of the continued breeding of Scottish Folds and some of the major cat registries, such as the International Feline Federation (FIFe) and the UK's Governing Council of the Cat Fancy (GCCF), do not recognize them.

CHARACTERISTICS
Coat
Most colours and patterns
Weight
2.7–5.9kg (6–13lb)
Lifespan
11–14 years
Personality
Sweet, affectionate, loyal, sociable
Origin
United Kingdom

ABOVE:
Owl-like
The small ears of Scottish Folds bend forward and downwards in the front of the head, giving them an owl-like appearance.

RIGHT
Genetic disease
Sadly, the mutation responsible for the cute folded ears in Scottish Folds also causes a genetic disease that affects cartilage and bone development.

LONGHAIR

ALL PHOTOGRAPHS:
Feline companions
Scottish Folds make great companions and can often be found snoozing on their backs and sitting with their legs stretched out and paws on their bellies.

LONGHAIR

407

Ears

BELOW:
Hearing
Cats are able to detect high-pitched sounds, such as squeaking mice, that we cannot hear. The external part of their large ears, called pinnae, can be moved independently, which helps them amplify and locate the sound. Some cats also have small hairs growing inside their ears, called ear furnishings, which are thought to help pick up faint sounds.

LEFT:
Unusual ears
Though most cats have upright ears, some are noted for having unusually shaped ears. Here, as a result of a genetic mutation, the Scottish fold has folded ears that bend forward and down towards the front of the head, giving the cat an 'owl-like' look.

BELOW:
Ear tufts
Some cats have longer hairs on the tips of their ears, known as ear tufts. Quite what these hairs are for is unknown. It is possible that they work like whiskers and detect objects above the head or improve hearing. This Maine Coon has both ear tufts and ear furnishings – hairs inside the ear.

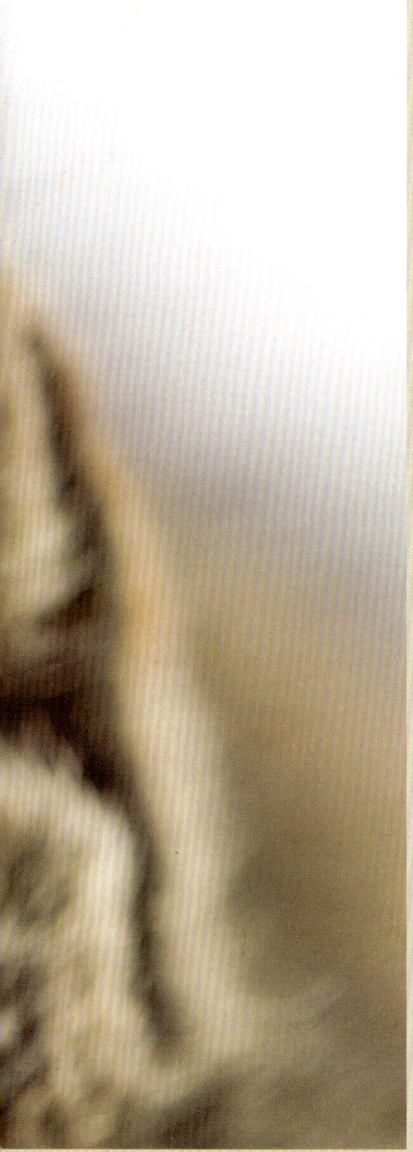

LONGHAIR

ABOVE:
Late curlers
While a curly-coated Selkirk Rex kitten is born with curly whiskers, the curls of its coat can take two years to fully develop.

Selkirk Rex

CHARACTERISTICS

Coat
All colours and patterns
Weight
4.1–7.3kg (9–16lbs)
Lifespan
10–15 years
Personality
Affectionate, easy-going, playful
Origin
United States

Named after the Selkirk Mountains, this breed's curly coat came about from a genetic mutation. It all started in the late 1980s, when a curly-coated female kitten was discovered among a normal litter in an animal shelter in Montana. She was later bred with a black Persian and produced kittens with long, loose curls, which laid the foundations for the Selkirk Rex. Himalayans and short-haired breeds – such as the British Shorthair and Exotic Shorthair – were used to develop both long- and shorthaired Selkirk Rex cats. Unlike other curly-coated breeds, the Selkirk Rex has a soft coat with erratic curls or waves and its curly whiskers break off easily.

But not only do the curly coats make the Selkirk Rex special. Affectionate and friendly, the Selkirk Rex tends to get along with everyone so is a great companion for just about anyone. It dislikes being left alone for long periods but thrives around its family, without being too demanding. Though Selkirk Rex cats are no trouble-makers, it is better to keep them entertained with toys as they can get bored. Its wonderful long coat needs regular grooming – but be gentle, you don't want to straighten those curls!

ABOVE:
Woolly sheep
The long coat of the Selkirk Rex has loose, untidy curls, which makes it resemble a woolly sheep. Typically, there are more curls around the cat's neck and belly.

Lovable personality
This cuddly curly-coated breed thankfully loves the attention and is happy curling up in laps.

LONGHAIR
Siberian

Also known as the Siberian Forest Cat, this rare breed with a thick triple coat, bushy tail and tufted paw pads is the national cat of Russia. Its ancestors come from the dense forests of Russia's Siberia, as its name suggests, as early as the Middle Ages. Long-haired Russian cats were first recorded in Russia in the 13th century, but the Siberian breed wasn't developed until the late 1980s.

In the 2020s, Siberian cats are gaining popularity for their magnificent looks and 'dog-like' personality. These sweet chirping-voiced cats are loyal to their owners, love to play and get involved in any household activity, and can be taught to walk on a lead – they are even fascinated by water and don't mind getting wet! Siberian cats are closely related to the Norwegian Forest Cats and, like these, are well adapted to extremely cold weather. However, Siberian cats have a three-layered coat (instead of two) to keep them warm. In spring, they shed their long, heavy winter coats, when the days become longer, and have a shorter, thinner summer coat for warmer months. And despite their long coat, some consider them to be hypoallergenic.

CHARACTERISTICS
Coat
All colours and patterns
Weight
4.5–9.1kg (10–20lb)
Lifespan
11-18 years
Personality
Friendly, playful, vocal, gentle, intelligent
Origin
Russia

ABOVE:
Pointed Siberian
Some cat registries, consider this colourpoint variety of the Siberian – with its distinctive blue eyes and dark markings – a separate breed under the name Neva Masquerade.

RIGHT:
Agile leaper
With its long, powerful back legs, the hefty Siberian can easily leap to exceptionally high spots.

LONGHAIR

Triple coat
Siberian cats are one of the fluffiest with their triple coats. The double-layered undercoat – awn hair and down hair – helps keep them warm during the harsh winters. The top coat, or guard hair, acts as a water-repellent.

BOTH PHOTOGRAPHS:
Weather-proof
Similar to the Norwegian Forest Cat, the strong and muscular Siberian is well adapted to harsh weather conditions.

Somali

With a long, bushy tail, this charming breed is essentially a long-haired version of the Abyssinian. Kittens with long coats have always appeared in Abyssinian litters, but these were initially rejected by breeders until the early 1960s. The US Cat Fanciers' Association (CFA) and The International Cat Association (TICA) accepted the Somali as a breed in 1979. Somalis are noted for their soft, fine-haired coat with ticking, where each hair has several bands of lighter and darker colour which gives them a shaded appearance. In fact, this finer coat – along with the slightly shorter wedged-shaped head and more rounded muzzle – has led the UK's Governing Council of the Cat Fancy (GCCF) to recognize the Somali Longhair separately from the Abyssinian. Like its Abyssinian cousin, the Somali is extremely lively and curious and will be up to no good if left alone for long. Often found on top of refrigerators or bookshelves to get a better view, no place ever goes unexplored and no task goes without help. Somalis are also very affectionate and constantly want to be in the company of others, though they generally do not like to be held. Their soft, semi-long coat requires regular grooming to keep it free from tangles.

CHARACTERISTICS

Coat
Ticked coat in various colours
Weight
3.6–5.4kg (8–12lb)
Lifespan
12–14 years
Personality
Curious, active, sociable
Origin
United States

LEFT:
Abyssinian descendant
Somali cats are named for Somalia in Africa, which borders Ethiopia – formerly Abyssinia – to show the connection between them and their ancestor, the Abyssinian.

ABOVE:
Fox cat
The sleek body, ruddy coat, large ears and bushy tail, have given the Somali the nickname fox cat.

LONGHAIR

Social manners
Somali kittens learn manners and appropriate behaviour from their mother, siblings, and other cats.

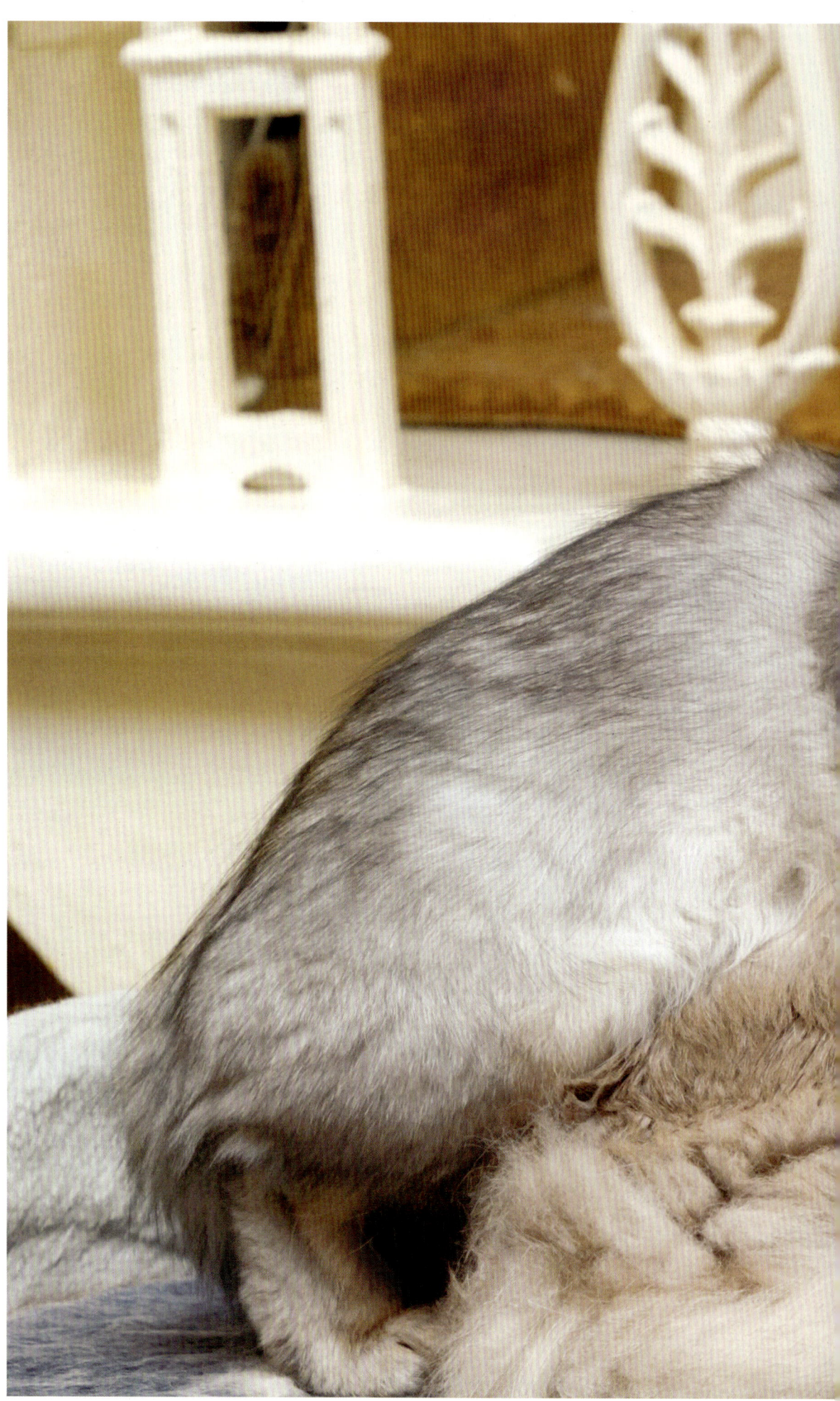

ALL PHOTOGRAPHS:
Bands of colour
Somalis have a very soft, fine-haired coat with ticking. Each hair has 4–20 different colours.

LONGHAIR
Tiffanie

CHARACTERISTICS

Coat
All colours; tabby and tortie patterns
Weight
3.6–6.8kg (8–15lb)
Lifespan
16–18 years
Personality
Gentle, curious, playful, sociable
Origin
United Kingdom

Not to be confused with the unrelated Chantilly-Tiffany, this striking breed was developed in the 1980s in the United Kingdom as a long-haired version of the Asian Shorthair. As it happens, Tiffanies were an accidental result of the Burmilla breeding programme that used the European Burmese and Persian Chinchilla. The Tiffanie was recognized by the UK's Governing Council of the Cat Fancy (GCCF) in 2003, but is not registered in any American cat registry. Those registries that recognize this cat do so separately under the name Tiffanie, or within the Asian Group as Tiffanie or Asian Longhair. The first Tiffanies were essentially long-haired Burmillas with shaded coats but now come in many colours and shades. Gentle and affectionate, Tiffanies are ideal pets for families that are mostly at home. These cats love attention but are not overly demanding and will happily chat, play – even by themselves with their own games – and cuddle with their owners.

ABOVE:
Silky coat
The Tiffanie's silky, long coat forms a ruff around the neck and a heavily-furnished plumed tail.

ABOVE:
Cold weather
Despite their long-haired coat and thick ruff, Tiffanies are not well suited to cold weather.

LONGHAIR

Yellow-green
Tiffanies are known for their big yellow-green eyes that are set well apart from each other.

LONGHAIR

LONGHAIR

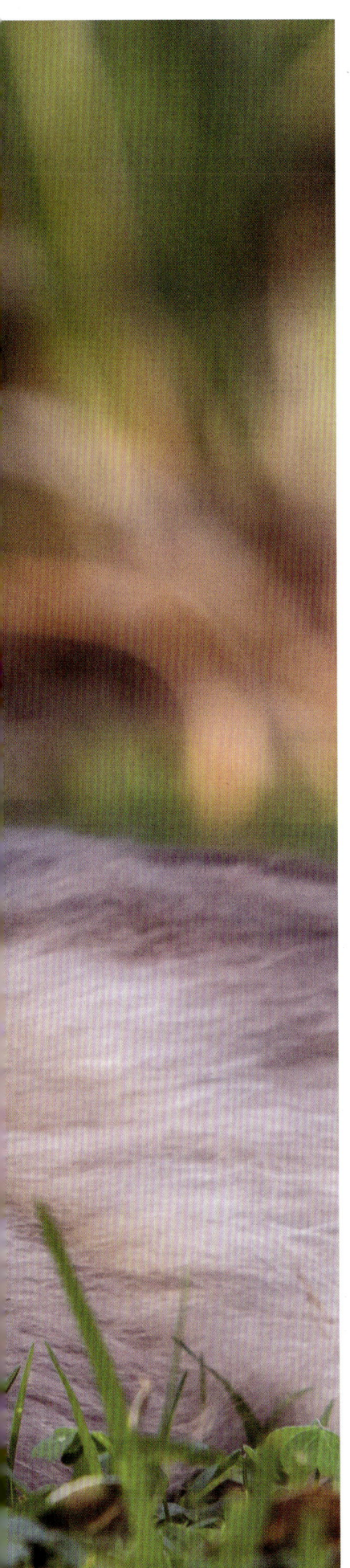

ALL PHOTOGRAPHS:
Happy accident
Tiffanies were an accidental result of the experimental breeding programme for the Asian cat called Burmilla.

LONGHAIR
Turkish Angora

This rare cat is native to the Ankara (once known as Angora) region of Turkey. According to legend, Turkish Angoras can be traced back to the Prophet Mohammad, founder of the Islamic faith, who once cut off his sleeve to avoid disturbing his beloved Angora cat sleeping on his robe.

By the late 16th century, this Turkish breed reached France and the United Kingdom, and quickly became a popular companion. However, it nearly disappeared in the early 20th century, when breeders used them to improve the coats of Persian cats. To preserve the breed, the Ankara Zoo established a breeding programme, where it continues to breed only white Angoras.

Despite its delicate appearance, the slender, ballerina-like Turkish Angora has a strong character and enjoys lots of family interaction. It may not always like to be held or cuddled, but it loves to play and retains a kitten-like energy into adulthood. With a streak of mischief, this attention-seeking cat should not be left alone much. While most often white, Turkish Angoras can come in many colours, shades and patterns. And no matter the colour, its single coat is always easy to groom.

CHARACTERISTICS

Coat
Many colours and patterns; most often white
Weight
2.3–4.5kg (5–10lb)
Lifespan
12–18 years
Personality
Energetic, sociable, playful, intelligent
Origin
Turkey

ABOVE:
National treasure
Turkish Angoras, a national treasure in their homeland, are more commonly white with blue or amber eyes. However, the most highly prized are those white cats that have one of each!

RIGHT
Ancient breed
This slender, silky-coated ancient breed from Turkey was the first long-haired cat seen in Western Europe around the 16th century, and for many years, all long-haired cats were called Angoras.

LONGHAIR

Fur variety
Although known for their shimmering white coat and bushy tail, Turkish Angoras come in many colours, shades and patterns.

LONGHAIR

ABOVE:
Random markings
A Turkish Van may have random markings over its body, but these are not as large as on its head and tail.

Turkish Van

CHARACTERISTICS

Coat
White with colour markings on head and tail

Weight
3.2–9.1kg (7–20lb)

Lifespan
13–17 years

Personality
Intelligent, affectionate, energetic, playful

Origin
Turkey/UK

This large, rare breed with a soft cashmere-like coat was developed in the United Kingdom, in the 1950s. Its ancestors, named after the Lake Van area of eastern Turkey, are said to have roamed southwestern Asia for hundreds of years. Turkish Vans have a white coat with distinctive colour markings only on their heads and tails, known as the *Van pattern*. However, a few registries also recognize all-white cats, without any markings, as Turkish Vans. And some even consider these as a separate breed called Turkish Vankedisi.

While it isn't likely to sit in your lap for long, the Turkish Van is an affectionate companion who can be petted or picked up from time to time. However, this zestful cat loves to climb, jump and explore, and is always ready for fun and games, especially if the family joins in. It even enjoys playing in water and will invite itself to share a shower or bath! When it does relax, the Turkish Van can be found in the highest places in an active home. Moderate grooming – except during the spring shed – is enough to keep its fur free from tangles.

ABOVE:
Mismatch
Turkish Vans are noted for their almond-shaped eyes that are often mismatched colours, with one being blue and the other amber.

LONGHAIR

Swimming cats
Unlike many cats, Turkish Vans love water and are known to be strong swimmers. This has earned them the nickname swimming cats. Historically, they even swam in Lake Van in Turkey!

LONGHAIR

Out and about
Named after the Lake Van region of eastern Turkey, these large cats with a soft cashmere-like coat were first developed in the United Kingdom in the 1950s.

LONGHAIR

York Chocolate

This friendly cat was named after its ancestor's dark chocolate-brown coat and the state of New York, where the breed was developed in 1983. The first York Chocolate, named Brownie, was born to two long-haired domestic farm cats – one black and the other black and white – with at least one of them having Siamese ancestry. In 1990, the Cat Fanciers' Federation (CFF) accepted the York Chocolate as an experimental breed, which was officially recognized two years later. A few other smaller or more recently founded breed organizations recognized this breed too. However, there are no longer any registered York Chocolate cats, nor known breeders, so the breed is considered extinct.

The York Chocolate, or York, was an affectionate companion that loved to be held and cuddled. While quite independent and active, this soft-voiced cat didn't like to be left alone for too long and was known to greet you or get your attention with its sweet motor-like purrs. York Chocolates also enjoyed following owners everywhere, often joining in with the household activities, and were always ready to play or snuggle up with the family.

LEFT:
Hunter
Quick and confident, a York Chocolate was a skilled hunter – mice didn't stand a chance!

ABOVE:
Coat colour
Kittens usually had a lighter coloured coat which would develop into a rich chocolate or lavender hue. Chocolates could also be white and chocolate or white and lavender.

CHARACTERISTICS

Coat
Chocolate, lavender, or bi-colour pattern (white and chocolate or lavender)
Weight
4.5–7.3kg (10–16lb)
Lifespan
13–15 years
Personality
Friendly, gentle, affectionate, intelligent
Origin
United States

OPPOSITE AND ABOVE:
Caring companion
The York Chocolate was an excellent companion that loved to play and be stroked or cuddled. It was also a great mouser that would keep gardens free from rodents.

Index of breeds

Abyssinian	10	Chartreux	94
American Burmese	20	Chausie	102
American Bobtail (longhair)	292	Cornish Rex	106
American Bobtail (shorthair)	16	Cymric	320
American Curl (longhair)	294	Devon Rex	110
American Curl (shorthair)	26	Donskoy	116
American Shorthair	32	Dragon Li	120
American Wirehair	38	Egyptian Mau	124
Aphrodite	42	European Burmese	128
Arabian Mau	46	European Shorthair	130
Australian Mist	54	Exotic Shorthair	136
Balinese	298	German Rex	140
Balinese-Javanese	338	Havana	146
Bambino	58	Highlander (longhair)	324
Bengal	62	Highlander (shorthair)	150
Birman	304	Himalayan	330
Bombay	72	Japanese Bobtail	154
Brazilian Shorthair	74	Kanaani	158
British Longhair	312	Khao Manee	162
British Shorthair	80	Kinkalow	342
Burmilla	88	Korat	168
California Spangled	92	Kurilian Bobtail (longhair)	346
Chantilly-Tiffany	316	Kurilian Bobtail (shorthair)	170

INDEX

LaPerm (longhair)	350
LaPerm (shorthair)	174
Lykoi	178
Maine Coon	352
Mandalay	182
Manx	184
Minuet	358
Munchkin (longhair)	366
Munchkin (shorthair)	188
Nebelung	370
Neva Masquerade	376
Norwegian Forest Cat	380
Ocicat	192
Oriental Longhair	384
Oriental Shorthair	196
Persian	388
Peterbald	202
Pixiebob	208
Ragamuffin	394
Ragdoll	398
Russian Blue	212
Savannah	218
Scottish Fold (longhair)	404
Scottish Fold (shorthair)	222
Selkirk Rex (longhair)	410
Selkirk Rex (shorthair)	228
Serengeti	232
Siamese	236
Siberian	414
Singapura	240
Snowshoe	248
Sokoke	252
Somali	420
Sphynx	256
Suphalak	260
Thai	268
Thai Lilac, Thai Blue Point or Lilac Point	264
Tiffanie	426
Tonkinese	272
Toybob	278
Toyger	280
Turkish Angora	432
Turkish Van	436
Ukrainian Levkoy	284
Ural Rex	288
York Chocolate	442

Picture Credits

Alamy: 6 (Perky Pets), 15 (ImageBroker), 53 (Loop Images Ltd), 111 (Lukasz Szczepanski), 124 (Astrid Harrisson), 125 & 127 bottom (MJ Photography), 149 (Imagebroker), 174 & 177 (Panino), 202 (Vivitaart), 203 (Jarosaw Kurek), 221 (ImageBroker), 227 (Yury Barsukov), 244 top (imageBroker), 245 top (EyeEm), 279 (Sipa US), 294 (Panther Media GmbH), 296/297 (Hemis), 320 (imageBroker), 322 (Abd Elilah Ouassif), 323 both (imageBroker), 324 (Susan Leggett), 326/327 (Idamini), 332 (Hulya Ozko), 366 (Heat Design), 395 (Sergey Sklezne), 420, 422/423 & 425 bottom (David Kilpatrick), 426 (Heat Design), 427 (Perky Pets), 430 (Chris de Blank), 440/441 (Andrew Linscott), 444 (Wirestock, Inc.)

Alamy/Dorling Kindersley: 54, 58, 60/61, 92, 208, 210, 211 top, 350, 367, 428/429

Alamy/Juniors Bildarchiv GmbH: 40, 114, 140, 144, 145, 156 both, 160 both, 161, 192, 340/341, 431 top, 443

Alamy/Tierfotoagentur: 141, 148, 159, 170, 171, 176, 204 top, 288, 289, 328/329, 347, 384 & 385, 410, 411

Licensed under the Creative Commons Attribution-Share Alike 3.0 International Licence: 20 (Heikki Siltala), 21 (Sergey Loubov), 260 (Maewboran), 264 (Tanyarae9), 431 bottom (Heikki Siltala)

Licensed under the Creative Commons Attribution-Share Alike 4.0 International Licence: 261 (Maewboran), 265 (Dreistone), 358 (William Parker)

Dreamstime: 10 (Anobis), 22 top (Namak), 36 (Tramp54), 38 (Slowmotiongli), 46 & 48/49 (Wirestock, Inc.), 50/51 (Fakharany312), 59 (Weeraworn Angchawala), 63 (Hellem), 71 bottom (Joytasa), 105 (Taniawild), 123 (Licao0415), 128 (Woff1966), 142/143 (Dizfoto1973), 152 top (Noonie), 154 (Slowmotiongli), 155 (22rus83), 162 (Pattanakesarat), 163 (Kimberrywood), 164/165 (Poco bw), 184 & 185 (Slowmotiongli), 193 (Natawien), 224/225 (Sintez), 234 (Serkucher), 238 & 239 (Ivonnewierink), 245 bottom (Juhajarvinen), 246 top (Davidtb), 246 bottom (Slowmotiongli), 255 (Walkingthedog), 266/267 (Dagmarhijmans), 313 (Feedough), 318/319 (Evdoha), 352 & 353 (FurryFritz), 370 & 374/375 (Vronivis1978), 380 (Puteli), 386 (Slowmotiongli), 392 (Ianmcglasham), 394 (Rmwmrwcawjrw), 398 (Lgbillman), 405 (Tychynska), 407 bottom (Murmu2005), 416/417 (Kathicof), 424 (Nelikz), 433 (Przekopm), 436 (Slowmotiongli)

Getty Images: 12 (anobis), 13 (shaunl), 91 bottom, 93 (Auscape), 112 (CasarsaGuru), 204 bottom & 207 bottom (Seregraff), 342-345 (Andrei Savin), 391 top (De Agostini), 437 (Anadolu Agency)

Shutterstock: 5 (Kutikova Ekaterina), 8 (namaki), 11 (Pixel Shot), 14 (Parris Blue Productions), 16 (OrangeGroup), 17 (iarecottonstudio), 18/19 (Ievgeniia Miroshnichenko), 22 bottom & 23 (namaki), 24 & 25 (Seregraff), 26 (Robert Way), 27 (Nitiphonphat), 28/29 (Jeanette Virginia Goh), 30/31 (Nitiphonphat), 32 (Lalandrew), 33 (HelloRF Zcool), 34/35 (Apisit Hrpp), 37 (Anurak Pongpatimet), 39 (Azovsky), 41 (Fernando Calmon), 42-45 (Oleksandr Volchanskyi), 47 (Heidi J), 52 (SeraphP), 55 (Atsunori Kikuchi), 56 (OrangeGroup), 57 (Daniel Thompson), 62 (Seregraff), 64 (shymar27), 65 (Eric Isselee), 66/67 (Alexander Evgenyevich), 68/69 (PaPicasso), 70 (Zanna Pesnina), 71 top (OlgaKan), 71 middle (mydegage), 72 & 73 (Viktor Sergeevich), 74 & 75 (Wirestock Creators), 76-78 (b marcos), 79 (Oak Tree Studiostock), 80 (FotoMirta), 81 (Chuangxin Zhou), 82 both (Photocreo Michal Bednarek), 83 (Natasha B), 84/85 (FotoMirta), 86/87 (AnnaDona), 88 (Thirawat Kayunkay), 89 (synchR), 90 & 91 top (JE Jevgenija), 94 (Katniss studio), 95 (DooBap), 96/97 (Tony Bowler), 98 top (anueing), 98 bottom (Shvaygert Ekaterina), 99 top (Akimova Tatiana), 99 bottom (GAyala), 100/101 (Zarin Andrey), 102 (flightofdeath), 103 & 104 (Anastasiia Chystokoliana), 106 & 107 (DragoNika), 108 top (Oleg Kozlov), 108 bottom (Slowmotiongli), 109 (Kolomenskaya Kseniya), 110 (Vilvarin), 113 (VH studio), 115 (OksanaSusoeva), 116 (Viachaslau Herostratos), 117 (kapichka), 118/119 (Yartseva), 120 & 121 (Jilin Su), 126 & 127 top (Artsilense), 129 (Viacheslav Lopatin), 130 (Johanna Mehrke Fotografie), 131 (Isabella Marlen), 132/133 (solar eclipse), 134 (helfei), 135 top (Isabella Marlen), 135 bottom (MD.Shaharial hasan), 136 & 137 (Pixel Shot), 138 (Wutlufaipy), 139 (andyyick), 146 (Yazkova), 147 (Svyatoslav Balan), 150 & 151 (Patrick Hatt), 152 bottom & 153 (Susan Leggett), 157 (slowmotiongli), 158 (Nikolina Ivanova), 166 (Maslowski Marcin), 167 (Nacho Mena), 168 & 169 (Gino Santa Maria), 172/173 (Nikolai Tsvetkov), 175 (Philippe Sonderegger), 178 (Cicafotos), 179 & 180 (Nynke van Holten), 181 (Jaroslaw Kurek), 182 & 183 (Sebastian Schuster), 186 (Dixon Photography), 187 (Atsupriatna24), 188 (Sviatoslav Shevchenko), 189 (otsphoto), 190 top (MDavidova), 190 bottom (SV zt), 191 (MDavidova), 194/195 (dien), 196 (VittoriaChe), 197 (Mary Tekushina), 198 (kukurund), 199 (Irina Nedikova), 200 (Glawe), 201 (Jenni Ferreira), 205 (Seregraff), 206 (Alina Troeva), 207 top (Ires003), 209 (Dmitry Gorodetsky), 211 bottom (Tanyakopets), 212 (Kamil Martinovsky), 213 (Review News), 214 top (Gita Kulinitch Studio), 214 bottom (Daydream Photographie), 215 (Review News), 216 (Bildagentur Zoonar GmbH), 217 (Dizfoto), 218 (Gennadiy), 219 (Pierre Aden), 220 (Kolomenskaya Kseniya), 222 (Andrey Tairov), 223 (iVazoUSky), 226 top (frank60), 226 bottom (zossia), 228 (Heidi Bollich), 229 (RynaKatte), 230/231 (Jagodka), 232, 233 & 235 (LTim), 236 (Viewvie), 237, 239 middle & 239 bottom (Ivonne Wierin), 240-243 (jojosmb), 244 bottom (Andrea Izzotti), 247 (fantom rd), 248 (Misha Leng), 249 (Kokhanchikov), 250 (EVasilieva), 251 (nevodka), 252 (Coulanges), 253 (omerfarukguler), 254 both (Chamod Lakshitha), 256 (Tanakorn Moolsarn), 257 (Alexander Piragis), 258 top (Seregraff), 258 bottom (tkach artvitae), 259 top (Cube pro), 259 bottom (Ollllga), 262/263 (Lus Kudritskaya), 268 (Andis Atvars), 269 (Cup Of Spring), 270 (phichak), 271 (Cup Of Spring), 272 (Sallye), 273 (slowmotiongli), 274/275 (dezy), 276/277 (Lifesummerlin), 278 (PolinaBright), 280-283 (Kutikova Ekaterina), 284 (Anna Krivitskaya), 285 (Ravelios), 286/287 (Anna Krivitskaya), 290 (seeseeie), 292 (AlexDonin), 293 (Andrey Prilutskiy), 295 (Jeanette Virginia Goh), 298 (Heidi Bollich), 299 (New Africa), 300 (SJ Allen), 301 (New Africa), 302/303 (Fazlyeva Kamilla), 304 & 305 (Borkin Vadim), 306/307 (Daydream Photographie), 308/309 (Nau Nau), 310 top (sophiecat), 310 bottom (David Bokuchava), 311 (Luxurious Ragdoll), 312 (Chuangxin Zhou), 314/315 (Dora Zett), 316 (Aykut Ozturk), 317 (JulieK2), 321 (Kelly Richardson Photo), 325 (Anne Richard), 330 (LensFoto35), 331 (ecuadorplanet), 333 (ML Photos), 334/335 (Beautifulblossom), 336/337 (Anne Richard), 338 (Monika Wroblewska), 339 (Slowmotiongli), 346 (Layla Fudashkina), 348 (Sergey Sklezne), 349 (Vershinin89), 351 (Philippe Sonderegger), 354 top (nikkytok), 354 bottom (nadia if), 355 (DragoNika), 356 (Seregraff), 357 (Nils Jacobi), 359-361 (Dave's Domestic Cats), 362/363 (Nneirda), 364 (Valeri Potapova), 365 top (Nils Jacobi), 365 bottom (fantom rd), 368/369 (samray), 371-373 (Henk Vrieselaar), 376 (Viktollio), 377 (Dmitry Naumov), 378/379 (Anastasia Vetkovskaya), 381 (Elisa Putti), 382 top (Astrid Gast), 383 (Elisa Putti), 387 (Heidi Bollich), 388 (Jong Chul Kim), 389 (Zanna Pesnina), 390 (Jacintne Udvarlaki), 391 bottom (Jasmine K), 393 (JulieK2), 396/397 (Richard345), 399 (Heidi Bollich), 400/401 (Yuval Helfman), 402 (Nynke van Holten), 403 (Serita Vossen), 404 (Azril Mansor), 406 (Artem Kursin), 407 top (Mariya Palagina), 408 (schankz), 409 top (YuryKara), 409 bottom (DenisNata), 412/413 (Eric Isselee), 414 (Pavel Sepi), 415 (Vvvita), 418 (Nikolay Shargin), 419 (Sleptsova), 421 (Heidi Bollich), 425 top (Coulanges), 432 (Helen Bloom), 434/435 (Nedim Bajramovic), 438/439 (Barrie Barrington), 442 & 445 (Ciprian Gherghias)